WITHOUT A CLOUD

Jon Picardi

This story is dedicated to my wife, Charlotte, and to my friends of course.

Phish in a Barrel, August, 6th

"Why did we want to leave Aberdeen so much?" I asked.

"We *still* do," said Phishy. "Just because you went to an almost out of state college doesn't mean mine or anyone else's dreams of adventure have been sated. I still want to bum around the world."

"Yeah, but why are we so passionate? It's all we would talk about in high school, between the inside jokes and references."

"It's boring here obviously."

"But we always had things to do—gaming, bike riding, kayaking. I just feel like it's not justified."

"I get ya. I think it was because of how easy this place is. There's no real crime, no real problems, no tigers in the bush, and no delinquent youths to tear shit up. We felt so safe, but I think we need some problems when we're young, so we have the ability to deal with them when we're older. That's why we undelinquents still needed to escape this heaven with video games and/or drugs and/or internet and/or sex and/or TV and/or breaking shit."

Ding ding ding dadong.

"You expecting anyone?" I asked at the sound of the doorbell.

"No, I'll be right back."

Phishy left his room and went down the stairs. I was curious so I got up and looked out the window to spy on our guest. There was a lone county sheriff car parked across the street.

My heart began to race; adrenaline rushed through my veins. When I heard Phishy open the door my blood caught on fire, but even with all of this chemical energy all I did was stand, immobilized.

"Raul Ortega," said the sheriff

"Yes?" said Phishy, confused.

The cop most likely said some catchy line or a roar of rage but I didn't stick around to hear it. I was so scared that everything slowed down into this gentle, fluid motion, like I was in bullet time. So in one probably clumsy motion, I opened the window, jumped onto the garage roof below, rolled onto the garbage cans in the backyard and over the fence into the construction yard around Phishy's house.

It was then that I heard the loudest noise in my life. It was one discharge from a shotgun. Into the chest of my friend, Raul "Phishy" Ortega. In hindsight, I don't think I was in any harm—all the sheriff really wanted was Phishy, but I was too scared to realize that. Or I was just trapped in a mindset that refused to let me think clearly.

Welcome to the Gunshow, May 16th

"All I'm saying is that the only problem with meth is that it doesn't kill fast enough."

"Really, Gunshow?" I asked. "Hundreds of people die from drugs and instead of helping them you're saying more should die?"

Beep.

"Yeah, well the war on drugs is shit. Everybody's still doing drugs and robbing houses to pay for them."

Beep.

"Young man, you need to watch what you say. You're working in public. I've been going to this grocery store for years and have never heard such language" said an old lady.

Beep.

Gunshow brushed back his flat, un-jelled mohawk and gave a small, snide smile. "Ma'am, I got Asperger's or some shit. I can't help it."

Beep, beep.

She almost jumped back in astonishment from the lack of apology. In her seventy years of life, no one had ever said anything else than "I'm sorry." It took her a moment to regain her authoritative composure. "I'm sorry. but I don't believe you," she replied

Beep.

"Your beliefs don't matter and they never will. I have it and you should apologize for offending my shitty autism." His voice matched her as-a-matter-of-fact tone.

Beep.

"Apologize to you? I'm the one who's offended! I want to speak to your manager!"

Beep.

"He's probably jerking it in his office so he's not going to side with you. But I got a paper in my pocket that'll shut you up."

Beep.

He reached into his pocket and pulled out a crumpled old note. Its writing was faint, possibly due to it being forgotten in the wash so much. The note looked so small clenched between his massive, freckled, hands. He handed it to her.

More freckle than flesh, Pete used to say. Gunshow never liked that statement. He always said "it's *all* flesh, you dickhead." But head to toe, Gunshow was covered in freckles. He was a ginger, just like his mother, older brother, and his Scottish ancestors that settled here. Gunshow had bright red hair that still had the faintest amount of dye from his "green" era. When he was a little interested in his appearance, it was sometimes jelled into a mowhawk. And during 90% of his life, it lay flat on his head. It almost covered up one of his green eyes, which somehow, were also covered in freckles.

Beep.

She read the note then cupped her hand over her mouth and winced very convincingly. She must have saved face a lot because she was very skilled. It's the only way to survive being easily offended after all of these years.

Beep.

"I'm so sorry, young man. I hope there is a cure for your affliction in the future."

"I don't," said Gunshow as he pushed up his chipped black glasses. He then calmly and carefully placed all of her products into paper bags. This was almost disturbingly bizarre, as his method for years was to simply shove everything in like a bank robbery.

Beep.

"The total is $54.07," I was finally able to say.

She paid and quickly walked away, somehow glaring at Gunshow even though she wasn't looking at him. She was possibly waiting for a good time to show her frustration and utter an old lady curse under her breath. Her husband was going to hear about this for weeks.

"Do you really have Asperger's?" I asked in an honestly interested tone.

"Da'fuck if I know," he replied. "My doctor thinks so and that's all I care about. This shit's great. It's like that note you give to your gym teacher so you don't have to work out, but for real life. I never have to be polite again."

"But you love working out. You can bench 435. And you're always wearing sleeveless shirts to show off."

"Yeah, but I'm empathizing with you. I work out seven days a week but you've only been there like twice or some shit."

"Yeah."

I looked away from him and out into the grocery store for any incoming customers, just in case I had to do my job some more. Gunshow became uncomfortable with the silence and let out a loud, exasperated whistle before he spoke up again.

"Yeah. So anyway," he said, "if there was a really bad batch of meth and it spread out over the city all of those fuckheads would die and crime would go down."

"Until the new methheads emerge and now there are more bodies," I said while still looking for customers.

"No, you misunderstand me. The drugs don't kill a little faster; after one hit the junkies drop dead. So the new people would be too scared to try meth," he said so loudly that I was forced to give him eye contact.

"I think they would still do it. People want drugs like that for other reasons, like depression or self-medication."

"Nah, I think some would do more productive shit, like write or paint or watch TV."

"Or swear."

Gunshow gave a wide, honest smile, revealing his chipped front tooth. "Fuck fuck fuck fuck fuck. Alright, no drugs for me today. Yeah, so some would then move on to heroin but make that shit kill too, and the next shit kill and the next shit kill. Then you got thousands of shitters dead, a couple dozen artsy-fuckers, the cartels fucked-over, and children free to roam the South-side like God intended."

"I still don't think killing lots of people for mankind is humane. I think these people can be saved too."

5

"Ah shit, you're right. Churchill and Roosevelt were such dumbasses. They should have put daisies on the panzers; then everything would have been better."

"Well *we* do drugs. Should we die too?"

"We're different; we do the lighter, more reasonable shit. Not the shit you know will ruin your life."

A chubby bald man walked up with nothing but eggs and light bulbs. He instantly knew what Gunshow and I were thinking so he looked around to avoid addressing it.

Beep.

"So how many people will die in your Utopia?" I asked.

Beep.

"I think if we had only two billion we would be good. We need a lot of people for genes and apocalypse shit. But not too much because then we'd have plenty of space and resources for everyone."

"$4.88. So would every country have a quota or something?"

"Nah, I like the idea of a game show."

The man paid but stood for a second and looked at us. He had the face of wanting to join our conversation, however, he decided to just leave. That was the best option because Gunshow probably would have told him to fuck off anyway.

"Ok then," I replied as I reorganized the candy above the conveyer belt.

"Speaking of murder-shows, how was college?" he asked.

"It was fun, and I'm nervous as hell for my senior year. My last year of school ever."

"Until every company deems bachelor degrees as worthless as high school ones."

"Yeah, I guess so."

"When did you get back?" He folded his arms and tilted his head backward. His authoritative stance revealed all of the wiggly arteries that supplied the blood to his melon-sized arms.

I grabbed the tie from my uniform and gave it a few squeezes, as I often did while thinking of something to say or do at work. "Yesterday I just wanted to be at home for a bit. That's why I didn't call."

"I guess that's cool. Did you know we're going to have a birthday party for Megan next Friday? Everyone's going to be there. It's going to be all weekend."

"Megan Foster?" I said with honest confusion.

"Yeah, she and her sister have kind of entered the group since God's party back in September. Laura's hot as fuck, and Meg's good too, but way too Christian for me." He smirked.

"I wouldn't think they were into our kind of party." I said with more confusion.

"Well, she said she wants one of 'our parties' to make her 21st more authentic."

"I'm going to assume Phishy's?"

Gunshow gave a loud "Ha." "Yeah, like we were going to have it anywhere else. So Friday is the regular dinking festivities. Saturday is going to be hanging out until the campfire at night. And Sunday is when Phishy kicks us out."

"I also assume I'm picking you up?"

"No shit, man. My brother's back so he's using the Bulletwagon."

"*Michael Rose and Brian Hessen to the manager office,*" creaked over the loudspeaker.

We marched over. I was shaking at the thought of what I could possibly say to keep my pointless minimum wage job. Meanwhile, Gunshow strutted down the store with his usual swagger. He used long strides with a big bouncy step to get to the manager's office at the back of the store. When we got to there, our manager, Raj was standing outside the door waiting for us in his sweaty manager shirt and extra short tie. Today's shirt stain was some brown masala. He raised his hand to stop me and gestured Gunshow into the office.

I didn't understand why Raj put up with Gunshow; at least twice a month a customer complained about his bedside manner. They worked together for three years; they must have been used to each other by now. It was probably that Raj

7

checked out another 'How to Manage' book and thought firing Gunshow was not the right way.

Gunshow's attitude stemmed from a long childhood of anger, sadness, and disappointment. He was the youngest of three brothers; of which the older two constantly picked on him. To escalate the situation, his father was the worst kind of alcoholic. Often the Old Rose would come home at three in the morning to smack his family over his progressive depression. His paychecks would go towards his hobby so the mother, Withered Rose, worked two jobs, which left the budding roses alone at home.

My friends and I avoided going over to the Rosebush, as Pete called it. However, Gunshow was always a procrastinator, so whenever we came to pick him up, we ended up staying an uncomfortably long time while Gunshow smelled which shirt had the least amount of BO. His brothers, Black Rose and Red Rose were always trying to question us on our heterosexuality due to our lack of girlfriends. If we did manage to have a female with us, they would hound her constantly for hang outs and illicit activities. When we fought them off, they retreated to snorting cocaine and casually watching porn together.

The awful family dynamic erupted when Old Rose went to jail. He had one too many bottles of rubbing alcohol or whatever he drank, and he pushed his luck on the road. A family of four were rushing to get Mom to the hospital for her third miracle when Old Rose stepped on the gas instead of the break and t-boned them at 70mph. None of the family survived. Old Rose broke everything below his waist, including his thorn.

It was a quick sentencing, and the Rosebush had one less problem...sort of. The situation didn't improve the other Roses lives but changed them. What was once a house of hate and rage became a house of silence and sadness. The family were refugees that finally found peace. And like so many refugees, the best thing they could feel was bittersweet. Withered Rose still had to work all the time, but she finally got a little respect from the boys. Todd "Black" Rose fell deeper into drugs and was now a homeless man somewhere in San

Francisco. Robbie "Red" Rose saw what happened to his older brother and joined the military. And Michael "Gunshow" Rose worked out all the time.

Gunshow came out of the office practically jumping. His smile was extra wide and his nametag was already in his hand. "Dude! I just got fired! Isn't that awesome?" he yelled.

"Well, it's not supposed to be," I replied.

"Now I can get unemployment and shit!" he said bouncing around.

"That's only if you're full time though."

"I know! I was! I told him to take a plane back to India then he yelled 'I'm from Pakistan' and kicked me out."

I stood up due to my nerves and said, "Wow. Well, unemployment isn't going to last forever. What are you going to do now that you've been fired from your only job history?"

"I don't give a fuck! Careers are for boring people. I don't give a fuck about being rich or whatever. And I don't give a fuck about accomplishing anything. And if I did I would go to Africa and hand out rice or some shit." He stepped back and forth to sedate his enthusiasm for his new found freedom.

"What about making money?" I stepped back and forth to sedate the nervousness for *my* potential new found freedom.

The black tie on his uniform was already undone, and his white collared shirt was already unbuttoned. He was working on removing his belt before he spoke up. "Fuck making money. I don't want to be a suit so why should I worry about dumb shit like money?"

Raj stepped out of his office to meet us. His arms were crossed behind his back and his face was more frowny than usual. Ignoring the half-naked body builder in his store, he looked right at me. "Mr. Hessen, please step into my office," said Raj with more breath than voice.

We walked in and I closed the door. He plopped into his chair and gave a deep sigh while he looked at some papers on his desk. The room had a faint smell of garbage and fast food. The carpet was covered in stains, with cans of energy drinks sprinkled upon it to create new ones. The walls were white except for a dark spot above the desk, probably where Raj put his feet up. The desk was supposed to look like wood, but the cheapness was so strong that the peeling vinyl simulacrum looked too fake for even fake wood. Behind Raj and the desk was a wall of overstuffed file cabinets with a dirty window on top. The chair Raj was sitting in was formally brown leather with the armrests shaved off from the constant rubbing of his arms. The burns and paint splotches implied that the chair formally existed somewhere else, in a more industrial setting. Why it spent its golden years in Raj's office was beyond me.

I sat down in the guest folding chair and looked at Raj. Sweat was pouring down his face and his tie was already undone. His hair was long gone and he was attempting to grow a mustache to reconcile, but he lacked the genes to do so. Instead, the thing below his long pointy nose resembled the facial hair of a post-menopausal Jehovah's Witness. Somehow his belly grew larger everyday despite most of his food getting caught in the corners of his mouth. With his sweaty little hands, he picked up the papers he was carefully looking at.

"So I see every time you are in trouble it is with Mr. Rose. I schedule you two apart but he always ends up at your register. I don't like him. I gave him the job because you told me he would be good. I understood he was your friend but he took advantage of us. Of you. He is fired already but I want to know what I'm going to do with you. So tell me, will you no longer get into trouble now that he is gone?"

I looked him straight in the eye. "Absolutely not. I will be a model employee."

He sat up in his chair. "Good. Then I'm going to promote you to a manager. Normally, I would wait until I have more availability from you because you're going back to school. However, I recently learned that I should not wait on a good opportunity. The position will pay one dollar more an hour and you will go from 25 hours of part time to 47 hours of full time."

"Wow, I—"

"Good. Then I will begin training you in two weeks, after I train the new-hires. You will need to wear a non-uniform tie and learn how our inventory system works."

"Uh, thank—"

"You're welcome. Now go finish your shift."

I walked out, stunned. Gunshow was already outside the grocery store waiting for me. His crusty, rusty, and busty bike was on the ground next to him. My mind was too busy falling apart to properly move my body, so my legs made more of a shuffle then a walk to meet him. As I passed the outside garbage, my locked-up face saw his work uniform stuffed inside—shirt, pants, tie and everything else. Where he kept his sleeveless-t and camo shorts combo he wore now was beyond my understanding.

When I got to him, he was head down, on his phone looking for people to hang out with. Unfortunately, everyone should be at work right now. "Hey, let's fuck this place and go get something to eat," he said.

As my confusion was reabsorbed back in to my body, I found the capability to speak. "Sorry, Raj told me to get back to work."

His head flew up with general astonishment. "What? Then why did he bring you into his office?"

"He told me you were a bad influence and I need to concentrate on my work."

Satisfied with my answer, he dropped his guard and picked up his bike. "Well, he's fucking right. So are you going to quit? Are you going to finally drop this duce after three years?"

I scanned the parking lot for any form of courage. I couldn't find any, so I couldn't bring myself to tell my friend that I was not as much of a bum as he was, and I will be spending less time with him. Instead, I squeezed out lie. "Well, uh, I don't know. I uh, would like some money. So I'm uh, going to reduce my hours to about uh, 15 a week."

He looked down at the ground and scuffed his shoe against the pavement. "Well that's cool, I guess. So I'll see you Thursday or some shit. Later, man."

"See you later."

Gunshow hopped on his bike and rode off. He had a little disappointment on his face but not too bad. At least he won his freedom; too bad I lost mine.

A Walk with God, June 5th

I lay awake in bed, staring at the posters on my walls. I saw heroes holding swords, guns, artifacts, beams of light and even a few women. Although as I thought about it, very few protagonists had women around their arms, even though saving them was usually the point of the game. It appeared like the prize at the end was so far removed from the actual game play experience that whatever happened at the end was irrelevant. As I reflected, the women in the games still seemed to be won, but more as a consultation prize for suffering so much as you saved the world. The damsels in distress were so irrelevant to the power fantasy that they easily could have been a keychain or some coupons. I couldn't answer this empirically though, because I've never met one game developer, and I probably never would.

Strange, I'd never met a celebrity either, so why was I so bothered by never meeting a game developer? Was it because I didn't care about the gossip industrial complex? Was it because I played these games so much? Maybe it was because I had a whole room covered with games but no movies or other media.

No, it was because I had no evidence that this industry existed. I knew it must, but I had no tangible proof. It was like meat: I knew it was an animal before, and it lived for years before it was killed. It must have had a mother and most likely a father, but I had no reference to it. In court I could only confirm that it was a sausage on a bun, and not an animal at any time.

I had no proof of these people, and the efforts involved in the creation of these products that I'd rather choose over sleep, school, and partying. At least I used to. Now I hung out with friends and did drugs. Now I blew all my money on booze instead of games. I would say that now I was socializing but I hung out with my friends more over multiplayer video games than I did today.

I also had better discussions while playing games. At parties, my friends would talk about shit we did before and shit we were going to do later. But before we would discuss why the Japanese and Americans would want to have hundreds of soldiers die just to take the enemy's flag, or how someone could reload when they had a gun in each hand, which would then drift into discussions of history, physics, and comedy.

I then thought about how events and ideas led into the next set of ideas and events, and those events inspired new ideas and events. Which made me wonder, was I my ideas or were my ideas me? Did I like games because I was a gamer, or was I a gamer because I liked games? Did everything I think I was occur before or after I defined it? I didn't think I liked games until I was given a gaming console for my birthday, but I only received it because some commercial said it was a popular item for children. Was my whole identity from some commercial I never saw? What about the commercial makers; did they design the commercial based on what they knew or what they were told? Was every thing's identity defined only from other ideas? But those previous ideas came from somewhere, so did ideas make new ideas like living things? And did we as sentient beings need to consume them like sausages?

Before overdosing on philosophy, I got out of bed. I promised God we would go apartment shopping.

Today I got this warm feeling from stepping on my bedroom carpet. I rubbed my toes in the formally green shag, catching fibers between them. I could feel how much this carpet just wanted to die already.

At school my dorm room floor was tile, which was a good idea because of all of the gross stuff that would fall on it. It was cold though, and it reminded me of a classroom—the coldest place of all. The decrepit shag reminded me of all lack of responsibilities I had. How much time that I could waste doing nothing. How much I could let everyone else be in charge of my own good again. How little I needed to care.

School remission was in full swing. My ears picked up the sound of a distant lawnmower. It hummed with the sound of relaxation, always accompanying me to my friends' houses for a day of splendid nothingness. My nose picked up the smell of the A/C. Its cool, chemical smell guided me back to all day game sessions in this very room. The sun peeked through the blinds, which was still plenty of light for my computer and TV-centric bedroom. The harsh light guided me back to memories of not needing a car even though I lived in the suburbs, because of the beautiful days that let me walk within them.

I got ready to go out. Nothing important happened. For the record, a lot of corners were cut, and I did enough as to not appear disrespectful, but not enough to be hygienic. I slipped my feet into my sandals and walked out the door.

The moment I stepped out I was blanketed in warmth. The feeling was so beautiful; it was comparable to a hot blanket on a subzero night. I knew this was only because of how cold the A/C made my house and in fifteen minutes I was going to want to go back inside. Such was the life of a human. I hoped God didn't want to walk around outside.

The breeze shook the trees as they applauded my walk down the street. I forgot how many there were. Every lawn had about four of them. And because the neighborhood was so old, a lot were huge—so huge that just a few trees could cover whole streets. The lawns were all green and semi-well-manicured, not like the yellow and brown grasses of the west.

The sidewalks were old, and every third one had a crack. None of them were level, and some were sunken so hard that grass and mud covered the splintering cement planes. It might sound like a bad neighborhood, but the depravity of the sidewalks gave a sort of authentic charm, like a hot dog joint that served drinks in little styrofoam cups.

The houses were old too. About half were built before the Titanic and about a quarter predated the Civil War. The Civil War ones were called signers because of the little plaque on the front of the homes that said: "This house dates to 18XX." The oldest one was an 1836 dream house, with two pickup truck-sized rooms and a potential for a stove addition. A family of 18 founded that house, because somehow Victorian Scotland was still worse.

The majesty of these old homes was seen in their uniqueness. 150 years of divergence gave some modern additions, like huge kitchens with tiny bedrooms or a half a house above the garage. Others were painted or refinished in fantastic greens, yellows, blues, reds, and browns. Some were brick, some were covered in plastic, some were still wood, some had garages, and some had sheds. A look at the houses' modifications could identify the last time the owners cared about them: plastic was post 9-11, garage was 80's, a caterpillar of additions in the back yard was 60's, a fence was 50's.

There were many different layouts too, with Victorian mansions, colonial cottages, plantation-like homesteads, and turn of the century (19th) craftsmen hovels.

A bike path ran through the town. It used to be a railroad, but trains were old news after WWII. It led through the Aberdeen Valley and all the way down to the Joliet prison. Walking down it always had the expectation of harassment from little girls with lemonade, but the smell from bakeries and butcher shops made up for it.

You always had to share with people walking their dogs, and usually the dogs were nice. The real problem was "on your left" with the aggressive bikers who were often too fat or old for their spandex. Dress for the skills you want, not the skills you have was the name of their game.

Leading into Main Street presented the shops—or what was left of them. On one side there was a tax place, a few empty buildings, a chocolate shop, a few empty buildings, an antique store, then all of the bars. The other side had a few empty buildings, a nice trendy restaurant, a few empty buildings, dry cleaners, a flower shop, the abandoned concert hall, then all of the other bars.

What could this place maintain with the thousands of middle-class shops to the west on Kirkman Road? Then what about to the east with the other thousands of middle-class shops in Luzern? And to the south were all of the pointlessly hi-end boutiques in Canterbury Hills. And finally, to the north was the

Super Amerimart in Victoria, with all of America ruining low prices?

God's house was on the hill just above Main Street. It was an old Victorian with ornate purple siding and gold trim. Six huge trees covered the lawn—well, some of it anyway. Random junk like toys, tools, and home improvement parts covered the rest of the unmowed lawn. There was a beautiful fountain with rusted spigots, dead leaves in the bowls, and fractured cement statues. It had rosebushes around it that once separated the fountain from the rest of the world, but now they swarmed the yard, tangling rusted toys from days gone by. On the porch, every step had its hole, and most were sagging into larger ones.

The Pelio's had a curse, which was that everything they owned broke—like the Midas touch with hulk hands. After years, a thick miasma formed and all inanimate objects felt this surmounting depression until they committed suicide.

Because walking was so perilous on the deck, I danced up the stairs, using muscle memory to dodge the pitfalls. I had to be careful too, because grass, old homework, wrappers, computer parts, and the 3rd microwave obstructed the holes.

I made it to the door and knocked. As usual, paint came off on my hand, a reminder that this house was updated around two children ago.

A little tan girl with big brown eyes and thick black hair opened the door. She was wearing boy's hand-me-downs that were five sizes too big for her. A year ago she would smile and hug me for a bit too long, but now she entered puberty, and the rules of engagement had changed. She stared at me, new found hormones trying to deal with yet another problem. The longer I waited, the more exponentially uncomfortable this moment was going to get.

"Hey, Thea, is God home?"

Her mind was too busy with the thought: *I don't know the things I want to do to you, but I want to do them.*

"C-can I come in and look for God myself?" I asked.

I pushed the door slightly and she dropped her hand, but she was still fucking staring. I wanted to just tell her "you're

17

seven years younger than me! I remember when you were in diapers! I don't find you attractive so stop forcing me to be creepy!" Saying this would make the situation legally too awkward so we resumed this game of cat and molestation charges. I took a step into the foyer as she ran up the stairs, yelling, "Sophia! Sophia!"

Some time passed until God finally emerged. She let out a huge yawn then rubbed her face as she walked down the steps—one at time of course. Her black curly hair was arranged in a hangover afro. Her big Coca-Cola bottle glasses were heavily askew, showing one dazed eye as twice the size of the other. Her pajamas were a repeating design of a video game logo from our childhood, but it was so faded it was hard to tell. The shirt portion was unbuttoned so badly that one of her breasts was almost exposed, but she weighed 90 pounds so it was just skin.

Every bone in her body could be seen with the naked eye, but because there was skin on top of it she didn't go to the hospital. Because she was not yet thinner than girls in the magazines, nobody worried about her. Except her mother of course, but she worried about everything.

"Jesus, Ammo. What time is it?" her voice squeaked out.

"Around one, I think," I replied.

"Oh, well why didn't you call?" she grumbled.

"Surprise!" I held out my arms like I just finished a dance and was expecting an applause.

"Ffff-fuck you," she said motionlessly *and* emotionlessly.

I noticed Theodora staring down at me from the top of the stairs. She was playing with her black blob of hair so aggressively that I was sure she was going to pull some out.

"Well uh, go hang out in Alex's room. I've got to get ready," said God.

"I'm pretty sure Alex is asleep too."

"Then I don't care, hang out with Nik, or my mom, or outside—"

"Or with me," exclaimed Theodora.

18

God gently turned around and crept up the stairs. What little of an ass she had was half out of her pants.

I went to the living room and saw Nik sitting on the only cushioned part of the couch. I brushed off a bunch of game controllers and sat on the opposite side of him. Theodora snuck around and sat between us.

Nik was 3rd of the four Peliolagos children—two years after God and six years ahead of Theodora. The oldest was Alex, but he didn't matter.

This year Nik transitioned from hoodie thug to popped-collar raver. His black hair was spiked with blond tips. His rose-colored indoor sunglasses matched his rose-colored popped-collar shirt. Of course the shirt was half unbuttoned, which revealed an extra hairy chest and noticeable man-cleavage.

The oversized TV was on but the sound was damaged years ago, so the subtitles were on the screen. A soccer game was playing. Nik would be interested but he was too busy texting. A corner of the screen was discolored from a magnet, so it made one of the pundits look like an old raisin.

I sunk my body into the fold-out part of the fold out couch and tried to get comfortable. Theodora being in her environment positioned herself accordingly, with legs folded like a movie star.

"Hey, Brian," said Nik. "Got any drugs? I'm going to a party tonight with my boys and need some good shit."

Theodora whipped her head back at me. Was she really dealing with a bad boy?

"You know anything like that I get from Phishy or Jerry," I replied.

"Well, give me their number," he said, still looking at his phone.

I laughed at him. "I know you don't have any money, and they're not going to give it to you for free."

"One of my boys can spot me."

"Then I'll give *him* the number."

"Fuck you, man. I knew you were a dick."

"Don't call him that!" said Theodora.

She knew her brother, and braced herself for whatever he was about to do to her. He did the usual grab of the shirt and yell routine.

"Shut up or I will throw you in your room! I will lock it! Then I'm going to beat up Brian!"

"You can't beat me," I said as I pulled his arm off her shirt.

"Yeah, I bench almost 200 and I was in excel gym."

"You were kicked out of school like, three years ago. All I've seen you do since then is smoke all of our weed."

"Whatever."

Then he got up and left, still texting someone; probably about how he's going to get some drugs from his sister's friends.

Theodora grabbed her shoulder and leaned closer to me. The smile she showed was small, but the smile on the inside was fifty times larger. "Thank you. My brother is so mean to me."

"Mm-hm," I said as I tried to brush her off.

I stayed glued to the TV, but I didn't know anything about soccer. There was no remote and I didn't want to get up to change it because I found the only comfortable position, and I knew she was staring at me. Two countries I never heard of were playing, one from South America and the other from Africa. One guy almost got touched so he did a back flip then grabbed his knee. I laughed a little but she laughed harder.

"Hey," said God.

I jumped up and spun around, awkwardness flying off me and splattering across the walls. God was standing behind the couch and was a little alarmed from just how fast I got up.

"So what do you want to do?" I asked.

"Well, I'm getting promoted soon, so me, Phishy, and Nik are planning to move into an apartment together. I found some places online and I want to check some of them out. "

"Are we going back to get my car? Or are we going to drive The Slag?" I asked.

"No, I think Nik took it somewhere. We can just walk; most are in Aberdeen anyway."

20

"Shit, I don't want to walk in this heat."

"Ammo, it's not so bad. We'll only go to the ones that are close. One's on Barnell Street, another is on Gunn Street, and the last is on Aberdeen Road," she said to me as she downloaded the day-ruining maps onto her phone.

"Aberdeen Road goes to Chicago." I sighed.

She scoffed and shook her head at me. "Shut up, Ammo. We're not leaving the town. Besides, it's so cold in here, the sunshine would be great."

"Can I come?" asked Theodora.

"No, Mom wants you to stay home and clean," declared God.

We left the house and headed back into the heat. The return to the outside brought the comforting heat burrito, but like a burrito, it betrayed me after a while. God was right beside me. She was in a good mood from actually having body heat again, along with her optimism for the future. God always felt that if she did just one little thing everything would be better— for her situation and for everyone else's.

She was well dressed for the occasion, Anorexia Nerd'osa in the summer. She had sneakers with little Japanese critters on them. Her pants were tight dark jeans, but since she had no curves, her legs resembled tiny denim tubes. She wore a tank top with some band I never heard of, probably from Phishy. She had dark hangover sunglasses that were almost a dark as her big black curly hair, which hung like a jungle canopy down her bony back.

"So we'll go to the one on Aberdeen Road," she said. "This one is pretty cool. It's right in downtown, on top of an Irish pub. From the pictures I got the feeling of that old-school charm."

"Is that the Irish place right on the river?"

"Yeah."

"I'm pretty sure it's way out of your price range. Even with Phishy's manufacturing job and Nik's whatever-he-does job. Ya'know, what does Nik do?"

"Well, Nik's unemployed right now, but Clatcher is going to do another hiring frenzy and Phishy is going to get him a job. And because of that we would be qualified for the Clatcher Housing Assistance Program. Any residence that's been refurbished by Clatcher would be cheap for us."

"Oh, I see."

Clatcher was the big assembly plant in Aberdeen. They made everything no one never thought about, like the tops to stick sifts, the clicky parts on pens, the metal wire in glasses, the actual switch on light switches, and other little uninteresting things. The big thing about them was their mission to restore Aberdeen to its wonderful glory. They would buy the broken down shops and homes and restore them to a husk with clean white rooms and brown plastic side paneling. If the buildings were a person, they would look like a Mormon lady with a jean skirt, just a little too conservative. Then Clatcher would turn around and sell them for very reasonable prices to their workers. They didn't just do this for Aberdeen either; Victoria also had restoration projects. This was a great idea, but Aberdeen's problem wasn't broken down buildings, it was its slide into irrelevancy.

"So what's the actual address?"

"11 Aberdeen."

"That's the one right on the corner."

"Yeah, right next to the concert hall."

The birds were chirping, the wind was blowing, and the occasional car drove down the street. I could point out a dozen things that were making noise, but for some reason everything felt so quiet.

"This sun is pretty bad," I commented.

"Ammo, you can't even feel it. Every twenty feet there's an oak tree that's bigger than my house."

"I don't need to see cancer to feel it."

She had to stop walking for that one "*Wow*. Okay, let's change the topic. How was school?"

"Awesome. I want you guys to meet my friends from out there, but they're all so far away. Most aren't even from Illinois."

"Very interesting. Are the parties like they are in the teen movies?" she said as she continued the walk beside me.

"I've told you about my school for years. Why do you care now?"

"Well, you're going to be a senior now so I want to pick out what you're going to miss before you miss it. I felt asking you what you're going to miss wouldn't be honest and you'll just tell me what I want to hear."

"That makes sense. So I guess my friends? I don't really care besides that."

"But you went to a world class school. People outside of the country know it. Aren't you going to miss being connected to something so big? Aren't you going to miss all of the culture?"

"No. I mean, the place is big but I don't see any culture. I don't see why I would miss being a part of a big organization. It's just an organization."

"But your school is bigger than Aberdeen! The town that you live in!" She brought out the hand gestures—something she did when she entered a debate.

"Russia is bigger than the US; should I move there?"

"That's not what I mean. Borders mean nothing except to the militaries that enforce them. I'm talking about what really is our modern version of tribes. Aren't you going to miss being a thread in the beautiful tapestry that is Illinois-Mississippi University?"

"No. I feel nothing for that place. I've had good times there but I'm not going to die for it, or even donate to it."

"Rouge planets have no sun, so they can't harbor life," she said.

"At least it wouldn't be so hot."

The conversation was cut short due to our arrival. Gully's was a trendy bar that boasted its own microbrewery and fancy dark ales. The inside had shiny brass pipes that stuck out of the old, crumbly, cultured bricks. Dark modern high tables with angular chairs took up half of the little restaurant. The other half was a new-yet-old bar with a bunch of beers I've never heard of lined along the wall. A Colorado and California Republic flag hung from the ceiling.

We walked up to the bar and looked for somebody to speak with. Nobody was in the building; no customers or employees.

"Ammo, look at all those bands!" The breath in her voice filled the air with dopamine.

The wall with the door had dozens of band posters and photographs. These were probably from the venue next door, before it closed down. Most of the memorabilia was of local bands that never took off. But a few were of bands that toured in Aberdeen before they got big, and a few big names that didn't know how small The River Blues Hall ended up being. There were so many posters that it took a while to identify them all.

A man emerged from somewhere. I didn't know how long he was standing behind us as we looked at the posters, but when God looked around she screamed. That was probably his usual introduction. He was chubby, with thin clothes that would only look flattering in God's size. He had big block glasses and a handlebar moustache, which seemed awkward with his inconsistently shaven beard.

"Hey," I said.

"Hey," he said back.

God gave a forceful swallow then said, "We're here about the apartment."

"Cool."

He went to the back and emerged with a set of keys. Without any acknowledgment, he shuffled past us and out the door. We ran out after him. His mental patient shuffle brought him to the back of the building where he unlocked a rusty cage door for us. It opened up to a small yard and a pathway that lead to a flight of old wooden stairs. He appeared to count each step as he went up. At the top, he unlocked a surprisingly new metal door into the apartment. Inside, he stood there like a damn mannequin, his face never changing away from the stupid customer service smile.

"Wow, it's so big!" said God.

"And bright," I replied.

"Yes," said the monkey.

24

The apartment was a large studio—about two-thirds as big as the restaurant below. At the entrance was a small hallway that led into a large room. The floor's wood was so brand new that it still left a dry construction smell in the air.

The walls were the same as the restaurant's below but with extra-shotty craftsmanship. The mortar was looser and even more crumbly. The bricks were uneven, and a few were jutting out. They all had cracks and chips.

The windows were new and about as tall as a person with a wingspan to match. They had a byzantine arch at the top with vertical bricks that were not 150-years-old. They were possibly from the 70's and had a more mechanical uniformity to them. There were five of them along two of the walls. The other walls didn't have anything but brick, but that didn't matter because the windows already let in so much light that the room was buried in amber. The only objects in the room were an old fridge with a heavy patina, a counter that went the length of one of the windowless walls, and a bean bag chair.

Back in the little hallway entrance, there was an old wooden door that led into the bathroom. The floor and one of the walls was the same as the outside room but covered in dust from the construction. The other three walls were made of a more modern dry wall that was ready for its first paint job. The light bulb was exposed at the top, and it did not fill the room with its penumbra. It cast long shadows on a seatless toilet, an old cheap sink, and a modern shower. The toilet looked like it wasn't white; probably light blue or green. The ring in the bowl implied it hadn't been used in years. The sink was rectangular so someone could rest objects on it, but the bowl of the sink was so big that only bottles in the shape of triangles would fit. The shower was a solid white plastic with a foggy glass door. It too hadn't been used in a while but showers don't need the attention.

"It said on the internet that it comes with assigned parking?" said God.

"Yes," said the dolt.

"Where is the lot?"

"By the gate in the back."

25

"I saw that it was 900 a month. Is that correct?"

"Yes."

There was a long silence.

"Alright," I said. "So we like this place but we're going to look at a few more. If we still think yours is the best, we'll give you a call."

"You will most likely here from us," said God.

"Ok," he said.

The apartment walkway led into a parking lot, which led into the riverfront walkway. The walkway was new—probably made to dress up Aberdeen and add to the list of family fun things to do here. Unfortunately, the path was built after air conditioning, cable TV, and the internet so there was only ever ten people on either side of this 3 mile long path on any given day. The only people who frequently used this path were old men that fish in the river and minors with no other form of transportation. The ground was made of brick and some were inscribed with names of patrons or people who contributed to Aberdeen's success. I wondered how many bricks the Clatcher family had. This path shouldn't be confused with the bike path, which was way busier and stretched from Woodstock to Joliet.

"So we're only going to one more, right?" I asked.

"I think we should see all of our options," replied God.

"What do you mean we? I'm not going to move in with you. Your bother is going to bitch about any place that's chosen, and Phishy is fine living in a box. You're the only one who cares and you really cared about that place."

"Yeah, that was a nice place but I don't want to make a wrong choice. This is a big deal."

We were quiet for a while as we walked down the path. She pulled out her phone again for the next location.

"So why did you hate that guy so much?" asked God. "I could see it on your face that you were very annoyed with him."

"He was annoying. Didn't say anything and didn't show us around. Unprofessional, I guess."

"Well, I like that he was more honest about his personality. Nobody likes a salesman."

"He wasn't honest; he was high."

"How do you know though? He didn't smell or act very strange. If anything, I would say he was only tired."

"No, he was high. High at work...he shouldn't be doing that."

"I think you're just mad because you're in this heat."

"And you're just happy because the apartment impressed you."

"Ok, then after this next walk-through we can go to your house or something."

"Good."

We walked down the river walk for a bit and noticed some tweens on their bikes smoking cigarettes. One tilted his head up like he knew us and God gave them a deep scowl. It was a while before she said anything.

"Hey, Ammo. Want to take a look at Graham Mansion?"

"Is it on the way?"

"Yes, if we walk past Graham Street and behind the grocery store we'll get to the apartment complex."

"Up the hill?" I complained

"Yes, now come on," she said with over-emphasized vowels of frustration

Aberdeen being a town inside of a river valley had some steep hills. On the steepest hill was Graham street. At the top of Graham Street was Graham Mansion. The very large mansion was constructed in the 1800's by the Graham family, who were Scottish industrialists that left the United Kingdom for the riches of the American frontier. The Graham's created the first factory in Aberdeen, a pottery factory that still existed today. And with their tycoon capitalism they created a massive stone home with dozens of rooms across multiple floors. However, it was not how the Graham family lived that was so interesting, but how they died, and how the house continued to get spookier as time went on.

We got to the top of the hill and God poked around the vine-covered walls and mossy wooden shutters. I maintained some distance, but I brushed my sandal against the crumbling stone pathway.

"Do you think we can get inside?" asked God. "I wonder if there's any spell books or torture devices in there."

"Well I heard the first floor caved into the basement, so no," I replied.

William Graham was a second son, so he always knew that it was up to him to achieve any success. With his hard edged personality and small fortune from his brother, he went to the middle of nowhere USA and built a factory. The reason he picked the isolated forest that was to become Aberdeen, was because his independent spirit made him mistrust everyone. And his ambition made him micromanage everyone because of it. He imported dozens of Scottish families and built his own alcohol-free, smut-free, and thought-free universe. He paid his workers not in dollars, but tokens that could only be used in his little town. He had strict control of all businesses that opened here, so only boring things like churches and taxidermists were built. William was the only one who made any actual money, and with his actual money he built the largest Mansion this side of the Appellation Mountains. This of course made the people of proto-Aberdeen very bitter to William.

God stepped on a moldy wooden crate, which gave her enough height to peer into the second story window. I walked up to her, but I was more cautious so I stayed on the ground.

"See anything interesting up there?" I asked.

"No. All I see are rusty metal bed frames. Well, I see a poster but it's too faded to read."

"There's a back door; you should try that."

"Good idea."

She hopped down and went to the backside of the house.

At one point, Willy imported a wife. And like the rest of humanity, she needed micromanaging and beatings to stay organized. Luckily, she was strong so she had two children before she died of alcoholism. Just days after her daughter Ashley was born, Mrs. William Graham was found dead in their fountain with a jug in her hand. Old Willy needed a person with active mammary glands for little Ashley, so she was raised by the only black person in the town, Edna. The older son, William 2, felt isolated by his mother's death and retreated into literature instead of capitalism like his father.

When Ashley became of age, she dated a black guy to piss of her controlling father. Her only true love was her milk brother Jeb, who eventually knocked her up. William ordered the baby to be executed and Jeb to be lynched. However, the town police hated him, so they blew him off. Old Willy had to do it himself.

"Wow, it's not locked!" said God.

"Well what would this place protect? Spiders?"

"I'm pretty sure there's something interesting in here."

The back door led into a kitchen, which must have been massive 200 years ago but today it was a little small. The counters were warped, rotten, and mossy with cabinets that anxiously awaited collapse. There was a missing space along the wall that probably housed the stove. In the corner was a 50's refrigerator slowly rusting into the floor.

"Not a lot of light gets in here," said God.

"Well, demons hate the light."

"Shut up, Ammo."

One night, William Graham invited Jeb over for a peace offering, but of course Will lied and blew Jeb away with a blunderbuss. Then Wet Willy went into the nursery and blasted the baby too. Ashley was horrified and resistant, but like every disobeying woman in the Victorian era, she was locked in the attic. She slit her neck on a broken window.

William Jr. also resisted his father but in a more sensitive way. He often wrote about poetry and did horrible things like advocate for the nearby Indians. Will 2 of course was heartbroken by what happened to his sister. He lost the only person who he could talk to about his feelings and parental abuse.

Will 2 read into dark magic and orchestrated a ritual in the back yard to resurrect Ashley. He sacrificed a virgin from town to allow his sister to enter the living world once again. It sort of worked, because in the coming days he wore elegant dresses and never left the Graham Mansion, just like his sister. On the 13th day after Ashley's death, Will 2 tried to slit Willy 1's throat while he slept. It would have worked too, but Willy 1 was an insomniac and caught him entering his chamber with a knife. Then he proceeded to beat Will 2 to death with a dirty chamber pot. Blood covered Will 2's over-tightened corset and silk floral gown.

"There's nothing in the fridge," said God

"Damn. I was hoping to get some pizza."

God carefully shut the fridge and walked over to the doorway into the next room.

"What's in the next room? Oh man, you were right about the collapsed floor."

I walked up to her and looked into the main room. The first floor was all over the basement, and wooden planks jutted out in every direction. The room looked more like a cartoonish pit of death than a decayed structure. The second floor looked as if it were about to join its lower brother; about half of the boards were snapped and slumped about a foot down. Some graffiti was on the walls, but the wallpaper was peeling like a wilting flower, and each tagged pedal gently fluttered into the basement.

"I don't think we're going to get much further," I said.

"Not this way; we should look into another first story window."

"Of course." I tried to give as little effort as possible as I followed her out of the kitchen.

The town was furious at the murder of the innocent girl for the Graham's dark ritual. They had no proof but due to the recent acts the only logical conclusion was that William Graham was Satan and needed to be killed. They formed a mob in front of the mansion, demanding that William give himself up. William instead called them fustilugs and fired into the crowd. He killed a person, but the mob was not deterred and stormed the mansion, knocking down priceless pieces of art that had been purchased off the labor of children. William had a full arsenal of pistols, blunderbusses, and muskets, and he used every one of them. A shootout ensued and Old Willy killed

30

about half a dozen people before the mob trapped him in his third floor study.

There was only one way in, and many windows to jump out of, so his plan was to blow up the door and fire into the crowd. Then when he was out of ammo, he would jump out of the window to safety. William grabbed a burning coal out of his fireplace with his bare hand and threw it at the door. It caught fire, but the burning proved too slow and Old Willy threw a bag of gunpowder at it, blowing it apart and killing a few more townspeople. He gunned down a few more but the survivors rushed in and stabbed William hundreds of times before he finally died.

"Hey, this room is still intact, and it has a creepy armoire. I bet William Graham Jr.'s dress is in there," said God.

"More likely a banshee," I replied.

God hopped through the window. I remained outside, looking on with a scowl.

She grabbed the door and tried to open it, but it was locked. She jiggled it harder and harder, but it wouldn't give. There was nothing in the small room but for an old mossy footstool. God picked it up and slammed it against the armoire. The door smashed into millions of pieces, and whatever spirits resided in this house should be on their way over.

God through her hands up in complete disgust. "Nothing! It's nothing! Why would they lock a closet for nothing? Stupid nothingness. Let's go, Ammo."

The army came in afterwards to keep everyone calm. The factory was sold to some wealthy businessmen from the east and the town moved on. The mansion was abandoned for a few years until it was reopened as a cholera infirmary, then a tuberculosis infirmary. Then it became an orphanage for delinquent boys. Then it became an insane asylum for violent patients until it was closed in the 80's for neglect. And when they were expanding a nearby road in the 90's, they realized the entire hill was on top of an Indian burial ground. So yeah, it was probably haunted.

We walked back to the street and God stared at the ground with her arms folded. A scowl was stuck on her face. I looked at her and knew I had to say something.

"What were you expecting?" I asked.

"I don't know, anything. Anything that could let me feel like this town is unique in some way. I mean how cool would it be if I found something in there that I could carry for the rest of my life? A something that connects me to my past because it could only have been found here and no place on Earth can replace it. Something that says my hometown is relevant and cultured and historical. Yet I found nothing, because nothing's here."

God's phone began to ring.

"What!" she said.

On the other end of the call was Nik, for only he could bitch and then be offended with one word. I could hear his whining through the craggily sounds of God's often dropped phone.

"Why didn't you bring me?" he asked, his voice muffled.

"I would have brought you if you stayed at home. You knew I was doing this but you drove off somewhere anyway," she replied.

"So? Why didn't you call me?"

"Why should I have to? You made it clear you were going to do something else."

"Then you should have waited for me!"

"No!"

"You're being an ass! I deserve to have a say in where I live!"

"Well I already looked at one place, but I'm on the way to the others. You can pick us up and I can hear your glorious opinion."

"Fine, but I want to see the one you saw already."

"Okay, Nik. After we look at the others. We're at the River Walk by the mansion. Come get us. Bye."

"Wait, I—"

God hung up the phone then gave me another Nik-tastic eye roll.

"Good luck," I chuckled out.

"What, you're not coming? But now you'll be out of this sun." Her body gestures now extended beyond her hands and her torso budged with every word.

"And into the Slag? More like out of the frying pan and into the fryer. And besides, I hate Nik. And he literally should not be driving without an adult." Her gestures spread to me and I was waving my hands as well.

"But I hate being alone with him. He's so annoying."

"Then forget about him."

"But I want to look at places," she whined

"We'll do it later. Let's go to my house."

"Fine. I never wanted him to come with anyway. If I didn't need his potential income then I would never move out with him. You want to play *Helltown 2: Hell Harder*?"

"As long as I play as Ghosts."

Clank, May 22nd

Phishy's neighborhood was known as the Fishbowl. Once a quarry, it was supposed to be the largest middle class neighborhood Kirkman had. However, the latest recession, depression, or economic situation (whatever the latest lack of money was being called) left much of it unfinished. So driving into this pit surrounded the traveler in a forgotten mess of construction.

There were square wooden house frame cobwebs standing still, waiting for walls that would never come. Large pits of prairie flowers waved at us as we drove by their big basement pits. Piles of home improvement store decorations were repurposed as homes for bees and chipmunks. And then the streetlamps that every night, at seven, reminded everyone what wasted potential looked like.

Phishy's house in particular was finished, which was a statement that should not need stating. For some reason, Mr. Ortega paid off the construction company a little extra to build his home on the express. I didn't get why he wanted it though; he must have known he would have woken up to construction every day for about four years. Maybe he predicted that building 700 homes at once was stupidly ambitious, and he would receive four square miles of privacy. Either way, the workers built a nice two-car garage home. I would describe it more but it could be found in every movie and commercial.

We arrived at the house and Gunshow and I stepped out of the car. It wasn't even two seconds before Gunshow opened his mouth to spew about something that pissed him off. I squinted, partly because I did not want to hear his dumb opinion and partly because the setting sun impaled my eyes with orange light.

"Ammo, why the fuck do you drive like a grandma?" he asked.

34

"Well there's deer and foxes running around this place. I don't want to hit one," I replied.

The real reason was that I was dreading this party. I hadn't seen my hometown friends in a while, and I didn't know what we could talk about. I was expecting to end up in the corner of the couch while they laughed at whatever they did over spring break without me.

It wasn't that they weren't inclusive or that I was subtly expelled from the group, but over the years at school, I had distanced myself from them. I was feeling like the people I had known for forever were sort of drifting behind me. I was a year away from graduating college and half of my friends had yet to apply. To me it felt as if they were in a loop of parties.

However, Megan and her sister Laura weren't really in the clique, so maybe the new blood would rejuvenate them.

"Goddamn, Ammo, you're always holding back. Just slam the fuckers. We could grill them up and make fox burgers." Said Gunshow.

"Well, I earned my nickname, same as you did, Gunshow."

"No shit. I should call you Brian again. See how much it pisses you off."

"Okay, *Michael*."

Gunshow shuddered. "That shit gives me shivers. Only teachers and doctors call me Michael."

When we got to the door, Gunshow had one of his 'I actually care about not offending people' moments. He stood tall and folded his freckled, pale and muscular arms as if he was about to lecture me.

"Hey, man. Before we knock, did you like, bring the Pedro Cali?" he asked.

"Yeah, but I don't know why you wanted me to get this for you. Megan's never had alcohol so she's not going to like tequila."

"Nah, it's for me; beer doesn't work fast enough."

"Well, if you have some needles I could try injecting it."

"Shut the fuck up." He paused and dropped his attitude. "So uh, when I uh, ya'know…" he said with a long hang at the end so I could finish his sentence.

It took me a moment to realize what he was asking. Gunshow was rarely sincere, so I knew his request either had to be about girls, booze, or lifting. We already went over the booze, and there was nothing to lift, so I had to think back to all the women he'd brought up since I got back.

"I'll make sure Laura doesn't see you vomit." I said.

"Thanks, and like, if you want my Mary Jane it's in your spare tire."

"Thanks, man."

"Just let whoever you share it with know it was from me."

When Gunshow rang the doorbell it was Megan's little sister, Laura, who answered. She was either 17 or 18 and had pretty brown hair with brown eyes that had yet to see any depth of life. She was a little tanner than Megan and a hell of a lot crazier, or so I was told. I barely knew either of them but Gunshow wouldn't shut up about what the Foster sisters had been doing with the group in the last year. She leaned a little too much on the door and smiled a little too hard to be greeting people in case a cop showed up. Her short shorts and loose top made me try really hard to remember if she was 18.

"Oh man, it's Brian and Michael!" she said in the best *Tonight Show* impersonation six Limón's could allow.

"Hey, Laura. Where's the birthday girl?" I asked.

"I think she's in the kitchen talking to Phishy and God. Watch out though, she might be blackout drunk after her first beer!"

Laura laughed too hard at the worst joke ever then stammered away, her beautiful body trying to make up for her comedy.

A party of my friends' was like a party on TV but without the good parts. We got shitfaced in a matter of minutes then tried to keep from passing out. We channeled our inner spirit animal and challenged the world and each other to a game of stupidity, daring each other to remember anything in the morning.

We played the games and had the conversations in the beginning. However, every drink reduced our group's mental capacity. As we stupefied, the conversations melted into grunts and the dozen words we could still recall.

Then the games surmounted into excuses to fuck up and laugh about it until one of the players spilled alcohol, vomited on the floor and/or the furniture and/or themselves. Halfway through the night, the situation devolved into gangs of unsupervised idiots, lurking and moaning. By the end it was a first-person-shooter, with bodies waiting to respawn in the morning.

Thank Goodness for video capture on phones, or most of my weekends after junior year would have been gone with years of schooling and only assumed fun to hold it together. Although this night in particular we had to put our phones into a box to protect a drunk Megan from being accidently posted on the internet. I supposed tomorrow we'd have to play the piece together game.

Entering from the front door was a hallway that led to almost every room on the first floor, and the stairs that lead to the next floor. Beside the second floor stairs and across from the door that led to the basement was a nightstand with the phone box on it.

Gunshow dropped his phone right away. He'd only had it for a few months but it was already covered in cracks and scratches. I checked my messages one more time before dropping my phone in.

Raj: "I know you're not trained yet but you will supervise Sunday night for inventory. Be there at 6 pm."

I sighed at the fact that I was going to pull an all-nighter after this but I replied with a yes.

Phishy's kitchen was large and white, like the kind of white that hurt people's eyes after looking too long. The granite countertops and stainless steel appliances proved Mrs. Ortega knew how to show her rich default lifestyle. Everything that should be wood was. Everything that should be organized on

37

the shelf was. Everything that should be so perfect as to be unnoticeable was. The only thing that sort of stood out was a big window to watch your kids grow up as you made apple pie from scratch. It almost felt strange seeing the 44 bottles of alcohol for our party. That wasn't cookie cutter.

Gunshow and I walked in on God, Phishy, and Megan having a conversation. Well, it was more of a series of words Phishy used to get God riled up.

Phishy knew what he was doing. He was leaned back against the counter with a beer in one hand, and the other placed over the few tiny hairs below his chin. Which aside from the two dozen above his lip, were the only hairs below his near non-existent eyebrows. Every so often he laughed, and the curly black rat's nest on his head would jiggle. However, aside from his big ball of hair, every feature on him was small. His lips, chin, nose, and cheeks were small enough that he resembled a shrunken head. It was up to his big ego to make up for his small features.

"So what, should we all be wearing rags?" said Phishy as he rolled his eyes.

God furrowed her brow and looked directly at Phishy. At this point, her hands were flying around with every syllable that fired out of her mouth.

"We don't have to be that extreme, but we should all move away from this shitty fashion industry. It teaches girls to feel as horrible as possible so they spend their money on garbage, only to be left in the dust next season when more stuff to buy comes out. Its exploitation made cool. Girls shouldn't want to be useless runway models but scientists or doctors, something that can better the world. Hell, a stay at home mom is more important than anyone in the fashion industry," declared God.

"Hey, guys," said Gunshow as he dropped his four bottles of vodka and two bottles of whisky on the counter.

"Hey, Gunshow; hey, Brian," Phishy, God, and Megan said in almost unison.

God assumed debate position now that there was a larger audience to hear her from her pulpit. She leaned in and spread her legs apart to make her 90-pound body as threatening as possible.

"It sickens me that we have a whole field dedicated to warping people's minds into depressed consumers. It's fucking worse than the drug industry; it's an abusive relationship. The worst parts of it, the biggest victims, are image concise people that love it and want to be a part of the machine. It's like *Brave New World*. Young girls have no hope against these monsters. Like Megan, what did you want to be growing up?"

"Well I uh, uh, I wanted to be an angel, to come down from heaven to save people and guide them to a better life."

We all stood there for a second, utterly dumbfounded as to why that of all things would come out of her mouth.

She stood there with a beer between her hands and against her chest, looking at all of us and wondering what she said wrong.

I knew her, but I never really looked at her. Her hair was the same wavy light brown as her sister, but while Laura's barely touched her neck, Megan's went halfway down her back. She had the same brown eyes as her sister, but there was something different about them. There was something hidden behind them, as if they had seen something else. She was shorter than everyone, but not abnormally so. She had the same face as her sister, except for a few freckles beneath her eyes. Her arms and legs were closed and as close to her body as possible.

"Well, what did you want to be after you couldn't be that?" God asked with a lot less enthusiasm.

"I still want to be that."

"No, like, what did you want to be here on Earth?" God said with some frustration.

She had to pause to think of something to say. Eventually something did come out. "A veterinarian. I wanted to save my dog, Sunday. And all of the other little kids' dogs. I wanted to prevent anyone from feeling my pain. I wanted to help people."

"You never thought about modeling?" said God, almost defeated.

"No, but I totally agree with you, Sophia. I think it's a horrible thing to hurt those girls like that."

"Well it looks like not every girl thinks like you do, God," said Phishy with a wide smile.

"I'm going to see what's up with Jerry and them because they're not talking about dumb shit," Gunshow said loudly.

"Wait, Gunshow, I bet you have an opinion of what women wear," said Phishy.

"Shit. I don't give a fuck what other people wear. More tits would be nice but I got porn. I will say this though, it's fucking stupid how those stores in the mall try to make men into women with fucking designer shirts and hair shit. They'll never sell shit, just piss men off. Like look at Phishy, he's gay as hell and still dresses like a broke asshole."

Aristotle walked out, leaving a horrified Meagan, embarrassed God, laughing Phishy, and me, not knowing what face to make. It took Phishy about thirty seconds to break the spell.

"Happy birthday, Meg." He laughed.

"I—are you gay, Raul?" said Megan.

"Uh, yeah," he said in his best queen bitch impersonation. Years of secretly watching teen girl shows had trained him well.

"That's totally fine. Really, I'm ok with that; you don't have to worry. I think it's cool. It's just that I didn't think you were a, uh, homosexual."

Phishy's eyes squinted as his tiny mouth curled into a handlebar moustache. Meg was firmly wrapped around his attention whore finger. He adjusted his little red glasses in preparation of his selfish mind-opening.

"Yeah, it's alright. As you can now see I'm not like other gay men. I don't care as much about fashion as God. I don't hit on everyman I see. I don't have a lisp, and I don't go clubbing."

"Oh, wow. That's really interesting," she replied.

God and I rolled our eyes. Phishy lived for this kind of thing, getting unsuspecting, now open minded people, to congratulate him on just being himself. Everywhere we went, he started up conversations with random people and every time it led up to his gayness and how he wasn't so gay about it. Every time they told him what a good boy he was for not being a stereotype. How nice it was for him to proudly wear nine-year-old jeans and a ratty metal shirt. How wonderful that he worked at a manufacturing plant instead of a boutique. How progressive his hobbies of drugs instead of fashion were. How exotic he was, being a twenty-one-year-old queer without a license.

Pete had a title for him: hipster-queer. And for the longest time Pete refused his gayness, calling it one of "Phishy's pointless plots." But just like everything with Phishy, it was and wasn't. It took two boyfriends and cheating with God's boyfriend to convince us of his slippery truth. In the end, Phishy got what he wanted: to make people feel open minded, and to feel proud of himself.

"I demand shots," our Lord decreed.

The three of them put down their beers and God picked up one of 50 hard liquor bottles. I grabbed five glasses and set them down loudly on the table; each one gave off the little clank that I considered the opening bells. Gunshow, hearing his theme music, walked in holding a massive gas station cup full of the fruit punch-tequila combo that he probably stole from Jerry. Tonight's opener was a clear drink from the cold harsh lands of Russia. God poured the bit and began the night. We raised our glasses and toasted another 21st birthday. Four clanks, then a brief pause for Megan. Then there was a subtle clank. Phishy poured the next round.

"Hey, can I get you guys later?" asked Megan. "I want to talk to the others."

"Yeah, Meg. We got it from here," said God.

There were clanks, then some talking, then four more clanks, then more talking, then only one clank, then small talk, then one more clank, then inside jokes only a ten-year-old relationship between four people could have, then one more clank. Gunshow stammered out, leaving Phishy, God, and I.

"What happened to Pete?" one of us asked.

"He still owes Ammo three bucks," another one of us replied.

They picked up their beers and resumed drinking. I walked over to the fridge to grab my own. The only option was Happy Henry's Hard Hooch, also known as cheap alcoholic pond water. I grabbed my lagoon juice and grimaced with every sip. God's buzzed brain picked up the conversation like it never paused. This was probably because she had a whole sluggish conversation in her own head.

"Ha, yeah, 'Ammo, ammo!' 'Ammo, ammo!' Remember World Divided?" God brought up.

"Shit, that game was only the best time I ever had in middle school," I said.

"Me too," said Phishy.

"Me too, minus the creepy guys," said the female one of us.

"Like, that guy that wouldn't let you pick up the flag without messaging him your tits," said Phishy.

"That was the day Pete made us use private chats," replied God.

"That was the *moment* Pete made us use private chats," I stated.

It got a lot quieter in that kitchen. Well, except for the blaring music down the hall and the people shouting over it. I looked through the big dumb window to see the backyard. The setting sun casted long shadows over the lawn where so many irresponsible bonfires were held. When we were children, God, Gunshow, Phishy, Pete, and I would calmly sit around that dangerous fire and tell ghost stories. Well, actually, Pete and I would make up the stories and the others would listen.

"But seriously, what really happened to him? I haven't seen him since the graduation party," said God.

"This always comes up. He just stopped asking to hang out, and got a new phone," said Phishy.

"But I miss him," she replied

"Yeah, me too," I said. "I used to ride my bike past his house sometimes; I thought about knocking."

"Why didn't you?" she asked.

"I don't know. I was going to, but after the first time I got cold feet for some reason. Every time after that, I still wanted to knock, but the feeling just got less and less intense. Now I don't really look at it."

"We should message him," said Phishy.

"Already tried a while ago; he doesn't respond," I said.

"Fuck, man; let's just go over there after the party," he said.

"I got work," I said.

"Then we'll do it later," she said.

"Yeah," I replied.

We all just stood there, each reliving a selected memory of our best friend. It didn't matter that he was probably fine and he probably didn't hold a grudge against us. Our poorly functioning minds each picked a memory to open and stare at. Every time we opened one, it brought us closer to Pete, but only to have the real him fly farther and farther away. We formed a trench of apathy with his laughs, jokes, insults, and gags. Every thought of him cut another groove, drilled a bit deeper, and widened the gap. Through all of this digging of the Marianas Trench, no one bothered to look up to see what pointless effort we had achieved. To just say hey, Pete, let's hang out. All we needed to do was build a bridge over nowhere so we could all make new memories.

I didn't know how long Dan was standing there, but he looked pretty scared. It must have been the silence. People don't like silence; opens up all of the seriousness. It's the opposite of alcohol, which can only encourage clear thoughts about your life, future to past. Silence forces a person to think critically of everything and make emotionless, logical, and difficult decisions. It's the shit nobody wants.

Dan didn't have any alcohol in his hands, which was unprecedented for him. He was constantly consuming liquor, and usually blacked out three or four hours into any social gathering. Whenever one of us brought up a drunk story, he would interject with something that truly disturbed us. Like how often he vomited blood or how often he woke up in strangers' beds. There was even one time he woke up naked, stuck in a slide at an elementary school, with his clothes in the river a mile away.

He was also a hefty guy—about 5'5 tall and 5'1 across. His neck, elbows, knuckles, and knees were hidden underneath rolls of fat. The back of his head also had fat rolls, which could only be seen because he had a buzzed haircut. His flesh was always pink and always sweaty. And he was always breathing out of his mouth when not drinking or eating.

"Uh…" said Dan.

God, like a mother annoyed with her kid, said, "What do you want, Dan? Do you need some water? Or pizza? Should we bring out the cake? Do you need a bed?"

"Don't let him on my bed!" said Phishy. "If he needs to relax put him outside! I'm sick of buying new shit because of his puke!"

"If you don't want this trouble, you should have said no to your house," God said in her 'negotiating with a toddler' voice.

"Ha, everyone knows we either do this shit at my house or nowhere at all; it's not like any of us are moved out or anything."

Dan's face jiggled back and forth between the arguers like a nervous zombie.

"Well when I get my promotion at Jake's Taco's, me, you, and Nik are going to get a place." declared God.

"You bring this up every time! We both know you're going nowhere until you blow Jake."

"Fuck you! I'm working almost forty-hours. Half the managers like me and would put in a good word."

"That sounds like something I heard five months ago!"

"Mmbeer please," mumbled Dan.

"Agh." God picked up a bottle and stormed out, handing it to Dan as she passed the doorway.

"Bitches, man. Right, Dan?" said Phishy. He took a swig from his beer and tucked in his tiny mouth underneath his top teeth.

"Yuh," he mumbled.

"That's why I like men. No fuss. Did you ever try men, Dan?"

"No, thank you."

Dan tried to turn away but his politeness was trapped in Phishy's snare. Phishy stepped away from the counter and over to Dan. He set down his beer and drew a devilish smile.

"Why not? You've never had a girlfriend and I don't think you're going to. You can try it out with me. I've been a lot of guy's first time's. I can go as slow as you need."

"No, thank you."

Dan's eye's screamed PANIC! But his body language mumbled "brains…" He winced and bit his lip as Phishy put his arm around him.

"Ah-hem. I can show you the world, a new fantastic point of view…"

"Ok, dude. Stop being an asshole," I said as I separated them.

"Well, you are what you eat."

Then Phishy trotted off with a smirk only girls with all the attention could have.

"Are you okay, Dan?" I asked.

"Yes, thank you." And we turned and walked out.

The Ortega living room had bottles and cans on every table, bench, and windowsill. The TV was on. Some young girl was walking on a beach with a frowney face. It had too much color for an anti-depressant ad, so it must have been about feminine products. Pink box. Yep, girl stuff. The minimalist mp3 player was hooked into a stereo system covered with stains from past parties. The music was loud and tinny, with the surviving speakers squeaking out some artist Phishy found a few days ago. Although the night was young, the house was already developing the alcohol/saliva smell. However, it didn't have that vomit tanginess yet.

There were the usual people: Gunshow, God, Phishy, Dan, Will, Jerry, Alex, and Nik, then we had some new people like the Foster sisters and around a dozen people I hadn't seen since high school (mostly Phishy's other cliques). We usually split up into three groups: the gamers, techies, and music/drug enthusiasts. I would bounce around each group until the conversations got stale. Sometimes someone came with me and by the end of the night everyone would have mixed around into a new group. Right now I wanted to start off with the drug group.

"Hey, Ammo, you heard Wisconsin is going to legalize pot?" asked Nik.

"Yeah, another reason to leave this shithole," I said.

"Well, the border is only like an hour away. We should do a road trip." He then spit on the floor and rubbed it out with his shoe.

"That would be cool but we need a place to stay, Nik. Also, I don't think you have the money." I said while trying hard to ignore his bile.

"Not if we ask Jerry to come with. We can all sleep in his van."

"The party bus? I don't want to sleep in that shaggy, grungy, 80's, ex-heroin den. I don't think it even works."

"Man, Ammo. You're such a lame ass bitch."

"Fuck you, Nik. You didn't even finish high school."

Nik shuddered; sweat began to bead in his greasy, spiked, Greek hair. There was a period of silence before Gunshow emerged with shot glasses and alcohol. He poured the shots and the conversation continued.

"Why do they call you Ammo, huh?" Nik asked. "That's a stupid nickname. Is it like, gay? Need guys to have sex with you and give you ammo in your ass? Why do some of you guys have these nicknames? Like, why is my sister named God? God is a man like in the bible. You guys are weird."

Clank.

"Because we have driver's licenses," I replied.

"Hey, man. Why do you have to be such a dick to me? I'm just trying to have a good time."

I held out my glass to Gunshow. Although he was doing the drunk dance, he poured my shot pretty well.

"Me too," I agreed.

46

I downed my shot and walked over to the gamer circle. More importantly, God was pouring some more vodka. After a few more clanks, I knew this was going to be a good party.

"I got this coconut oil and it doesn't work right."

"I'm sorry, ma'am. What was the problem?" I asked.

"I bought it and it's all waxy. They must have not sealed it well at the factory."

"That is how it is when it's dry, ma'am. It needs to be heated up into oil."

"I don't think that's right."

"I'm sorry, ma'am. Do you have a receipt?"

"Don't get snippy with me, young man. You shouldn't be rude to your customers."

"I'm sorry, ma'am. Do you have a receipt?"

"No. But can't you look it up on the computer? Maybe on the Facebook? My granddaughter put me on there. My name is Eunice Inglehoffer."

"Wh—no, I can't see that on Facebook. I can look you up on our records though. When did you make your purchase?"

"It was on a Wednesday. Wednesday is the day I always go to the grocery store because Dick goes golfing with his cronies. I think it was before his birthday, so it must have been a little while."

"Do you know the date?"

"It was around the 4th."

"That was more than 15 days ago. Our return policy does not go beyond 15 days."

"What? Well Pig Tails has a 30-day return policy."

"That's nice. Ours is 15."

"Well, I'm just an old lady and I can't keep track of my days. Could you just do me a favor and refund me?"

"I can't."

"Well then, I want to speak to your manager!"

"I am the manager."

"Well, I want to speak to your supervisor."

"He is not in. I'm the one in charge."

"Well then, I want to speak to your corporate representative."

"It is Sunday; our corporate offices are closed. I can take a message for you."

"Okay, my name is Eunice—"

"Oh no, that's okay. I got all your information on the store Facebook."

"Good."

I was really earning that extra dollar an hour now! And I got to better the lives of my favorite customers! Waiting to close on Sunday night allowed me to reflect on all of the wonderful things the customers had told me. It's like a teeth-grinding highlight reel.

"This is too expensive."

"Do you price match gas stations?"

"I'm too old to make any hormones so I'm just a cranky bitch."

"Do you guys have this obscure product I've only seen in Korea?"

"Your bag boy has too many tattoos, he should be fired."

"Your squeaky carts gave my child autism. I want a discount."

"What do you mean I can't smoke in here? I thought this was America! Land of the free? More like land of the nannies!"

Being a manger provided so many responsibilities! I was accomplishing so much! Most importantly, now that I was a manager I had no one to throw the problems up to! Instead I had to dump my problems onto my employees.

"Hey, can I get the number and maybe address of that cashier girl? The one with the glasses? I know her mother or something."

"Hey, man. Can I sleep here?"

"I'm an asshole, can I get a discount?"

"But if I didn't push you so hard then you wouldn't achieve anything."

Being paid to be annoyed was wonderful! What was I going to do with my extra dollar? Maybe I'd get a cheeseburger, maybe a nice pack of gum, maybe I'd save it and in 60 years I'd get a car.

Squish, May 23rd

The light was harsh. The gentle ebb and flow of the light's penumbra reviled boxes, old game systems, and CDs. This wasted space must have been the basement. Out of the corner of my eye I saw that the TV was on. It was paused on one of my favorite childhood cartoons about the harsh lessons of growing up as a pink dragon. The glass table between the TV and couch had a dozen hard liquor bottles. Some of them were tipped over with most of the hooch on the floor. I recognized the couch. It was the Franken-couch, made from cushions found on dumpster dives around the valley. The memories made my hangover feel a little better.

With my newfound energy, I attempted to lift my face off the concrete floor. Unfortunately, it was stuck. Being an experienced binge drinker, I whispered, "Fuck." Fortunately, my mind was still straddled from the hangover, so complex thoughts like "Why did I let this happen?" and "I need to perform some serious self-loathing" couldn't get in the way. It would be a while before the philosophy and understanding lobes kicked in.

It was then that my body was online just enough for the senses and I realized that my right eye was locked shut. My updated nose gave me the final motivation to rip my head off the ground.

It was so fast that pieces flew I'm sure, but I was too terrified to look. I moved my body like a surgeon's knife, slowly revealing the state I put myself in. It was dry, but not too dry—like overnight chili. It was all over the floor and on half of my face, with significant portions jammed into the holes that produced taste and smell. A quick look at my clothes revealed my shirt was compromised, but my pants remained unscathed. I noticed that I had my pants off at some point because they were unzipped and my belt was undone. There were plenty of alcohol stains on them. My final moments must have been trying to put them back on.

I strategically removed my shirt as small globs fell to the floor. After that, I used the shirt to wipe off most of the chunks, but I spread more than I removed. I dropped my shirt on the floor, and some of it splattered around. I decided this was as far as I was going to get without washing, so I crept slowly up the stairs.

I stepped as stiffly as possible; every tremor jiggled another piece onto the brand new wood. It still creaked like it was as old as Queen Victoria though. I bet the basement still had that new construction smell. Too bad I couldn't smell it. I shook again, and a chunk fell right on the railing. Even in this darkness, I knew because I grabbed it. I could feel it curl between my fingers.

I reached the top, and with my dry hand I opened the door. I would say it was bright, but that was an understatement. My eyes were adjusted to the one dim light down below, and combined with my top ten worst hangovers, it was more of an incineration of the retina. It was like I had opened my eyes for the first time.

It was almost silent upstairs, except for the buzzing of the stereo ready to play Phishy's indie of the week. My belt was jingling though, sticking out from my belly. I gave out a little whimper, as anyone who was encased in their own juices would. I had one sandal on, and it made a shuffling noise along the floor. As I lurked closer to the bathroom, I began to hear snoring.

The door felt sorry for me and gently went to the side as I walked in. This wasn't the first time it was so generous.

Being the house of a woman who secretly had no interest in style, it only had two restroom themes to choose from: nautical and French. This one was French. A poster of 19th century French cat food hung beside a big mirror with a red shawl underneath nostalgic amber lighting. The shawl drifted all the way down to a black and faux marble sink. The sink came with a cheap Eiffel tower thing, matching French word toothbrush holder-soap dispenser combo, and Fleur-du-

Lis towels. The toilet had a matching marble seat, along with a tissue box that had little ads of Victorian era French stuff. The Piece de Résistance was the Chat Noir shower curtain, but it could not be seen under Gunshow.

Gunshow was passed out in the shower, snoring almost as loud as he talked. Phishy's black cat Miyazaki rested on his chest. She looked comfortable, gently bobbing up and down to Gunshow's dragon roars. His shirt was rolled up all the way up to his chin, and his pants were undone but not off. The shower curtain was underneath him, and it looked like he attempted to make a blanket out of it. As per tradition, his glasses were gone to the last place anyone would ever find them—most likely with another piece broken off. I would have liked to use the shower but I knew nothing could wake him out of his Odin sleep.

I turned on the sink but quickly realized it was clogged, probably from Gunshow. There was a bathroom on the top floor of the house, but it was too far. I didn't want to actually be seen like this. Again. I especially didn't want to be seen by Megan; she wouldn't know how to react. As embarrassing as it was, the only option was the toilet.

I got down on my knees and moved my paws around for a cup. Gunshow was never more than five feet from an empty one. What I found near his hand on the floor was a giant plastic cup from a gas station.

I carefully lifted the lid for the tank and tried to get a scoop of the water, but the coma-inducing sized soft-drink cup couldn't be angled to get any more water than a spoonful. I put the tank lid back on with only a few smears and got on my knees. I prayed to the only true God(s) and lifted the lid. Everything looked normal. I scooped out a good amount of water, moved my head over the bowl, and dumped it. The water ran down my face, and I could taste it all over again. *Flush*. Again. Another taste—good thing my stomach was still empty. *Flush*. Not as much this time. Again. *Flush*, almost nothing now. Again.

"Are you drinking out of the toilet?"

I whipped my head at the door, eyes wide, water dripping off my whiskers. This was the worst-case scenario:

Megan. Mountains crumbled, empires fell, and sea levels rose before I even remembered how to speak. As my synapses moved at a snail's pace, I settled on the second worst answer: "Yes."

"Why?" she asked with a face of more curiosity than disgust.

Why indeed? It would have been less embarrassing to have stayed in that basement forever, Hendrix style. However, if I told her no, she would learn about the *Phantom of the Opera* vomit mask that was on my face. Somewhere I decided that some lie could put me in a better light, for she was a person who had never experienced the morning after a party. Then I realized I could use that to my sort of advantage.

"Yeah well, I just woke up and needed some water. The sink was kind of clogged so I used the toilet. I heard they're cleaner than sinks anyway."

She looked confused and sad, like I was supposed to say something else. She must have smelled right through my lie. That didn't matter because she squatted down and rubbed my back. She winced for something to say to me. "Where's your shirt?"

"I, uh, don't know." I couldn't look her in the eye so I fiddled with the cup.

"Oh, Brian. Are you still drunk?"

"Y-Yes."

"I think I am too. It's ok, right? Everybody does things they regret when they drink. Isn't it part of the package? It never amounts to anything, right?"

I tossed the cup aside so I could comfort her with the eye contact from a disgusting man. Her eyes glistened with more emotion then she was letting on.

Fuck, why didn't I die? Why didn't I die?

Now they were getting red.

"These situations, they're just the flavor of life, right? We drink 'till we wake up then laugh about what must have happened. We tell our friends, children, and grandchildren and it doesn't reflect on our character? These nights are only temporary?" she asked as a tear drop fell onto my pants.

"Of course, these nights are all about fun relaxation. We drink like this so we are all equal, connected. This is the time to bond and forget our thoughts."

"Yeah, our thoughts are just too heavy."

"'Da fuck smells like shit?" Gunshow made a massive roar, even for him, as he plopped half of his body over the tub. Miyazaki leapt off and coolly walked out the door. Gunshow hid half of his face on the side of the tub, exposing half of his disorientation. "What the fuck do you guys want?" he said, in pain.

"Nothing?" I responded.

"Shit, then go fucking shower or some shit. Just get the fuck out of here." Then he closed his eyes and returned to the gentle golem state.

"Well then, I'm going to shower. Megan, I'll see you in a few minutes," I said faster than a 1920's news anchor. Then I got up and walked out, not even looking to see what face she was making.

The rest of the house was a mess; cups and bottles everywhere, people on the floor, furniture askew, and a sticky film on the floor from the alcohol. Upstairs was better: just clumps of vomit on the carpet and knocked over pictures. Phishy's bedroom was open, with Dan on the floor, pants off and someone else on the bed. It couldn't be Phishy though; someone else always sneaked into his bed before he ever got the chance.

The bathroom upstairs was nautical, with a bunch of beauty products on the counter and in the shower. I dropped what was left of my clothes and stepped in. The hot water instantly released my problems and I began to think of what clothes I could borrow from Phishy's dad. I thought it would be the faded Florida Keys tank with sweatpants-shorts—the ones with paint all over them.

No Right on Green, May 23rd

Eugene Kirkman was supposed to be some unheard of farmer. Just like all the ones around him. Just like all of the ones before him and after him. That's not to say farmers should never become famous or achieve great things, but Kirkman did not live his life striving for success. It might have been different if his family acknowledged the money and dropped the farmer mentality. However, his old lady could still be seen mowing the grass around the farmhouse with a pipe held up by the scowl of her face. The house itself was dutifully maintained, but it was nothing spectacular—especially for one of the richest ladies in Illinois. Although the kids showed up in their Ferraris, she still drove an old 60's Caddie. Although the kids wore designer clothes, she still wore a worn out green sweater. Although the kids were constantly on their phones, she only used a landline. When the old man was still around, not much was different except the Ferraris were seen less often in the gravel driveway.

I didn't know if the Old Kirkman's regretted their decision, but even whizzing past the house at 60 mph, you could feel her spite, her rage, her calloused deposition.

I wondered how often she dreamt of starting off on her normal Saturday morning mow, when suddenly she bumped off the curb and crossed 11 lanes of traffic at a blazing, rage-fueled 6 mph. Her withered frown would vibrate slightly as she ground up all of the yuppie shoppers and the fuckups that worked in their stores.

She would sneak up on the jogging women with their overpriced headphones and knock them over. Her steed would splatter blood everywhere while the little white headphones that cost them their lives wrapped around and around the blades.

She would find a group of orange girls and their queer friend staring at their phones. She would sneak up to them on her riding lawnmower, engine roaring with insanity. One of them would say, "This phone sucks. The vibrate is way too loud." "You should get the new one," another would say. Then the first one would respond, "Yeah, I should." Then BAM! They would scream "OMGwhy?" and "lolsorandom" as they were sucked into her red vortex.

Next would be the shops of plastic and kale. Her crusader wagon would bust through the glass, sending shards all over the plants and shitty furniture. A stoned skeleton with bags under her eyes would say, "Ma'am, you need to park that outside," but the Old One would grind her up like a bone saw, chunks hitting the blenders, which would somehow made xylophone noises. After her beautiful portrait of catharsis spread across miles and miles of Kirkman road, she would return to her lawn, her scowl never lifted, even though she reached ecstasy for the first time.

Or maybe I picked up some of her fury as I drove past her.

Kirkman was a bitch if you didn't know how to exactly get where you were going. The road itself went for miles through Illinois farmland, connecting Wisconsin and Missouri. The awful part was a little four-mile stretch of road in the heart of the town. It was supposed to have every shop you needed. However, no one could reach them because there was no order to the stores or even a map to plot the landmarks. So one was left with remembering all the times they were lost until they figured out where they should be. Eventually, muscle memory led to the little desired store until—gods forbid—you wanted to go somewhere else. It's horrible, but it could have been a little easier if the turns and side roads weren't all brilliantly or stupidly designed to trap someone once they made the decision to actually turn off Kirkman into one of the other store sections.

Each section was about the size of a city block, with a bunch of random stores arranged in randomly shaped strip malls and a few random standalone out-of-the-box stores floating around the randomly shaped parking lots. Each store block was isolated by the store blocks next to them; usually by a field, a runoff ditch, a manmade lake, a row of trees, or just a really high curb. Then the realization would set in that, "Hey, I thought this was the block that had my store but I was mistaken.

57

If only I could see anything smaller than a warehouse from the road."

The left (or sinister) turn signal took about two minutes before it let anything back on Kirkman to try again. Often the right-turners still had to wait for the light anyway without the benefit of the traffic computer caring about them. The never-ending traffic of the main road would fry anyone's patience who dared to turn right into the ice cream or hamburger store.

Kirkman was west of Aberdeen, and it was the last town in Chicago's sphere of influence. After that last example of modern suburban living was rural Illinois. Which was home to people with gentle southern accents living in spontaneous towns surrounded by farm fields. Sometimes the madness of Kirkman rd. flung a driver west to this often ignored land. The only symptom of their situation was the subtle change of shops to large warehouses, and then to even larger warehouses, and then nothing.

This whole problem was multiplied again by the fact that the town of Kirkman was designed for cars, not people. There were no sidewalks, no bus stops, and no urban density. The little winding hairs that fringed off the main drag wiggled around open fields for miles. Until the roads reached big blobs of clone houses arranged as if they were surrounded by history and culture, and needed to squeeze in as much space for the five bedrooms and fenced-in back yard. Unfortunately for all those involved, those neighborhoods became paint splatters across the map of corn. Any entertainment or sustenance for its residents was a dozen minutes or so away by car, so TV and pizza delivery ruled the 'hoods.

The agoraphobic enclaves lacked anything within them as well. Children sentenced to live there seldom left their cells. The new blood tried the outdoors, riding their bikes down the looping empty streets, searching for any stimulation. After the failed quest, they too retired to their boxes with the lesson that the only contact came from a phone, and the only entertainment came from a screen. Occasionally there was a small tree in someone's yard, to let a lone bird chirp through the silence of a land with allegedly hundreds of people living there.

I was driving through this mess because I was the most experienced to suffer it, like a sailor chosen because of his sinking experience. William-san and Megan were with us, but they hung out in their respective towns, so it would have been worse with them. God came as well, but she always convinced someone else to make decisions, like drive on her behalf. So with no one else yet awake after the party, I was it. I was the lamb that was to drive through the Valley of the Shadow of Death. I was pissed but the four of us wanted food after a night of hard partying, and the closest food by the Fish bowl was on this shitty road.

We were also in the worst possible situation. We wanted diner food and God remembered a nice chain diner some guy took her to but she didn't know where it was. We were all hungry and getting more stressed with each passing failure.

"I don't understand. The GPS said that the place was right here," said William-san.

"Gps's don't know Kirkman. Nobody knows Kirkman," I replied.

"I'm pretty sure a lot of people know Kirkman. Like city planners and civil engineers," retorted God.

My eyebrows furrowed from her stupid answer. "Nobody planned this crap! This whole town was made by some guy in New York with a degree in confusing people until they buy something."

"Calm down, Ammo," said God. "You're driving too fast."

"No! I'm not going fast enough!"

"Why don't we try this Italian restaurant?" Megan calmly suggested.

"But I want pancakes," said God.

"I've spent all of this time looking for the stupid diner so we're going to find it!" I yelled.

"I got my signal back! Okay, it's going to be the next right. The biggest store should be a grocery store," William stated.

I pulled in and drove down to the parking lot, but there was no grocery store to be found. Instead, the biggest store was an adult toy store next to a *very* adult toy store. I didn't move the car until William-san's phone had another bright idea.

Settling in the parking lot, I could see that the clear sky let the sun burn the pavement until the heat visibly distorted the air around it. The cars and shoppers wiggled through the lens of this extraordinarily hot day. Now that I had calmed down from my distraction, I looked back at Will for another false direction.

He was a rather nerdy looking guy; collared, button-up shirts with fancy bow ties were his style. A tilted trilby or fedora often covered his head. And white-framed glasses almost the size as God's said his geekiness was on point. He was an actual nerd too, for he loved anime, manga, and video games. However, when people tend to see an African American man dressed like a dork, they just think he's fashionable.

"Okay, maybe this is actually it," he said. "Take a right then in two blocks then take another right."

Like a guided missile, I flew to the phone's next location with everyone desperately gripping their respective handles. As I whipped right, the tires screamed at me to stop, giving a voice to my silent passengers. My aggression was fruitless however, because yet again this was the wrong place. At least that grocery store was here.

"Maybe it was on the other side," said William. "Try taking a left."

I jumped to the left turn lane. The red sideways middle-finger otherwise known as the red left turn signal gave me time to relax and think about what was most important in my life, I guessed.

"William, are you sure you entered the right name for the restaurant?" asked Megan.

"Yeah, remember I showed everybody? I don't know why it keeps failing us."

"Every time we use technology is just another opportunity for it to disappoint us," declared God.

"That's an interesting point, Sophia," said Megan innocently.

"I can agree, but I think technology makes everything better," said Will.

"Well, tech failures are only going to get worse. I'm pretty sure some error will annihilate our civilization," said God.

"We could use a physical failsafe," said Willy.

"What?" asked God.

"Let's say in the future some computer controls all of our money. Then an error pops up wanting to delete everything along with all of the backups. Well, to do that some guy will have to physically unplug something, and then walk somewhere and physically complete the final execution. The computer can't do it without him. It's like the Odysseus and the siren story."

"I suppose that works, but people don't usually have that kind of foresight. I don't think humans would do something like that ahead of time," replied God.

"Well, I think a little higher of human engineering," he replied

"Is that what you're going to college for? Technology?" asked Megan.

"Heh, well I am a fan of that stuff—especially sci-fi. I'm actually in school for Architecture. I plan on moving to Japan and teaching English for a bit while I get my design portfolio in order. After I prove that I can live in Japan and create elegant designs, I should hopefully get into an architecture firm. Then eventually I will create the most Avant Garde structures in the world. After that entirely new cities around the world will follow my model. Well, that's what I hope for."

"Very interesting. When do you plan on moving?" Megan asked.

"I don't know. Soon, I guess? I have my degree and enough money from my graduation party. I'll go when I'm ready."

The light changed. I whipped out. The philosophy ended. Everyone held tight. I could feel the car tip. If we were in an SUV, I think we would have rolled.

I turned into the next parking lot but again there was no diner, just another superstore, some boutiques, and an authentic Mexican restaurant. I had enough of this negation navigation so I pulled in front of the restaurant. After my episode, everyone else agreed.

Although the building was made of a plain tan brick on the outside, the inside was decorated in authentic Latin American colors. The tables had pink, yellow and green cloths atop older wooden benches. The walls were covered in Mexican memorabilia, from the flag, to the map, to the giant mural of a young couple in extravagant clothes dancing with a bowl of fruit. Whatever part of the wall that wasn't covered by nationalism either had a bright, colorful tapestry or musical instruments. There were three floor to ceiling windows that had paintings of flowers, eagles, another flag, and lots of food. Altogether, the paintings blocked a lot of the sunlight, so the amber lights within the restaurant gave a low, relaxed atmosphere.

At the counter was the daughter, who seemed to be at the state college level in her life so this little hole in the wall was beneath her. She was chewing gum, and as we approached, her mouth increased in noise—no doubt to alert us of her actual status and the contempt she felt towards her peasant family.

"What do you want?" she asked.

"A table for four please," said God.

"Sit wherever."

Looking around, the only other customer was the sweaty father speaking Spanish on his phone. He had the face of a man negotiating to prevent a bad conversation with his wife. We sat down at a table as far away from him as possible.

Megan looked down at the table, and then at the sauce bottles. It was the standard green and red bottles with the salt and pepper inside of the alcohol bottles. She then looked up at us, trying to see the menu from the counter, since we didn't think the daughter would come to our table.

"So, Sophia," said Megan. "Why do people call you God?"

"Oh, heh, yeah. I'm sorry if that offends you," God replied.

"No, no. I'm just interested."

"Well, we had a friend named Pete and he used to hang out with us. He was the one who gave me the nick name."

"Oh, I remember him from high school. But why did he give you that name?"

The daughter showed up after all. She dumped the menus on me and stared at us for drink orders.

"Iced tea."

"Doc Smooth."

"Fitzlemon."

"Iced tea."

She walked off, phone in hand.

"I can answer that." I cleared my throat for the speech. "So we used to play a game called World Divided together. In it we had respective rolls we all played. Gunshow—I mean Michael—was the 'vanguard.' He would charge in without strategy or reason and attacked whomever he wanted. Our jobs usually consisted of us trying to keep him from getting killed. Pete was the assault, going in but with some intelligence, and often getting the most kills. Phish—Raul—was the assassin, going in full stealth and actually taking the objective. I was the support/sniper. I held back and sniped until someone, usually Pete or Phishy, needed ammo. Finally, uh, Sophia was the commander. She drove around in the vehicles giving us orders."

"But why God?"

God sunk her head back in embarrassment. I didn't understand why she wouldn't want me to explain a character trait she had that someone could learn in a five minute conversation with her.

"We didn't elect ourselves into these names. Pete assigned them. So when she started giving orders to us Pete would sarcastically say, 'Yes, princess.' Then when that got annoying even for him he said 'yes my queen' then 'yes, my Goddess,' until he shortened it to 'yes, God.' The rest of us called her whatever he did during this time."

"So it was all from just a game?" asked Megan.

I took a sip of my Doc Smooth. "I don't know. It was starting out, but we've called each other that in real life for years now, even though we don't see him anymore. He had a way of figuring someone out—a way of figuring *everything* out. He had this knack of identifying patterns and then calling someone out on it. He was always thinking about everything, and was always so chill about it."

Megan and Will sipped their drinks in complete enthrallment. Naturally, this was a question they both had for a long time now. Meanwhile, God gulped down half the calories she was going to consume that day. She also threw her hands around like she was debating. A silent protest, I supposed.

"You guys learned so much about yourselves from a video game," Megan said

"Well, he did about us. And it's a great way to learn," I replied.

"Wouldn't real life be better though?" She held her hand up like she was offering something to me. That must have been some defense mechanism to keep me from getting upset.

I took a gulp of Doc. "No, because in real life people are always in some façade, or looking to get something out of someone else. In a video game, everyone is more chill and anonymous, so people let themselves out. Just because the medium isn't real doesn't mean the people aren't. Besides, I don't understand why people have to bash video games. It's not the games that keep kids inside, it's the adult supervision and the adult ideas of what are good for children that keep them in."

"Hey, Ammo. You're getting a little off track," said God.

"Sorry, I'm just so hungry. It's pissing me off. When did she bring the drinks? I didn't even get to order my food."

"You were really in your discussion so I ordered you a burrito," she replied.

I drank some more. Good, I preferred someone else taking control of my decisions for a while.

Sniff, May 23rd

Nobody knew what Phishy's dad did. We asked Phishy once and all he said was, "something with warehouses." Normally, a parent's occupation held no interest to us. They went away during the day, we came over, and then they came home in the afternoon. The only reason we asked was because of Phishy's fire pit. In the backyard was a stack of 8-foot high wooden boxes his father brought home occasionally, and we would subsequently burn them on weekends.

They burned great. Rarely did we have to scour the Fish bowl for branches and twigs. They could get pretty scary at times though. People expect a fire to be low to the ground and manageable, not a towering inferno a few feet away. When we burned two at once the heat was unbearable. Anyone that tried to adjust the blaze entered an 80's action movie of grunts and anguish, complete with environmental aggression against completing the objective. Tonight we were smart and only burned one at a time.

The fire pit itself was only that: a pit—a hole with dirt—surrounded by patchy grass. The rest of the backyard could be seen from any lawn care commercial, complete with white picket fence.

Even though the sun had not yet set, this Saturday night was already the perfect night for a campfire. The air was a cool and calm breeze that could persuade anyone into bundling up into his or her old high school hoodie.

Gunshow and I were the self elected pyro technicians of the backyard. He moved the first pine sacrifice over the ash pit. Then I preformed the ritual of pouring too much lighter fluid around the sides of the box. Gunshow used the ceremonial lighter. It was once a pink candle lighter, but it was covered in so much grime from our parties that it resembled some beer-battered fish stick.

Whoosh, the fire lit up and we gazed upon our success.

We were silently standing there, not a word to each other, which didn't feel right. We didn't say anything before, when we were setting it up, but that was because we were in machine mode. This silence was a little different; a little crack in our wall of oblivious pleasure. This was the first moment of the weekend where we retired our levity for anything of meaning. Our minds were ready for any self-reflection that would complete this opportune moment. But then our peers exited the building before any thought could be provoked.

They came out in groups—most likely the ones they were discussing nothing in. The veterans went to the garage for their assigned seats. The folding cloth chairs with cup holders always went first, and the rest had to deal with plastic chairs that could only be found at a school gymnasium. One by one, they placed their chairs around the campfire while continuing their conversations of bands selling out and the latest happening on some show. Finally, when they were all situated around the fire, Gunshow and I sat in the chairs we grabbed before we started the incineration.

"Hey, Phishy," said Will. "I just realized, where did your parents go this weekend?"

"Some aunt died in El Salvador so they went back to see her. They'll be back Monday," he replied.

"Also, didn't you used to live in Victoria? I think I remember you on my bus."

"Well, I live here now."

"Will, don't you know every person born south of Texas lives in Victoria?" said Gunshow.

"EL OH EL, Gunshow. You're so fucking funny," replied Phishy.

"Yer damn right."

Gunshow tilted back and took a few gulps from his spiced rum jug. I wasn't sure if he was aware of Phishy's sarcasm. Either way, he owned the situation.

"So do you guys sing campfire songs?" asked Laura.

I suppose too many seconds had passed since anyone noticed her.

66

"Nah, we usually talk about nothing. Like, hey Jerry, isn't your van haunted?" asked Nik.

Jerry's sharp blue eyes may have stared at the fire, but his mind was clearly in another plane of existence. His right hand played with the holes at the end of his faded blue hoodie. His left hand rested behind his head, which prevented the static of the chair from frizzing out his blond shaggy mop of a hairstyle.

When Nik called him again, he jumped out of his nirvana and readjusted himself. He leaned forward and put one hand in what remained of his hoodie pocket while the other fixed his hair and the blond mess known as his beard. After his face was clear, the hand fixed his overly-distilled ripped jeans and disintegrating hoodie.

"Yeah, it was crazy as hell. So when we were coming back from Lolla I felt a hand jerk my steering wheel and we almost crashed into some homeless guy. The dude about shit himself," said Jerry.

"Maybe it was the mushrooms?" asked Laura.

"Mushrooms wouldn't do that to me. And I didn't do any until we got on 90."

"Are you sure nobody just jerked the wheel to scare you?" asked God.

"Nah, Will was sitting next to me and he's too much of a boy scout to pull some shit like that. And everyone else couldn't reach from the back. Shit was too spooky for me."

"What did you do about it?" asked Laura.

"Nothing. I guess I should have burned some incense."

"That would scare me so bad. I think I would have to get a new car," she replied.

"No way, man. I could never give up the party van. The van's got a couch, two recliners, optional table, and a TV. A TV that I personally brought in from the 21st century."

"And it has stains on 90% of the carpet and drapes," said Will.

"I'm going to clean it. I'm just waiting until I go on my cross country road trip. The first stop is going to be Madison, where I'm going to roll the fattest blunt and smoke some legal shit at a café. I'm basically going to be the first overdose of marijuana."

"You're going all over the country?" asked Nik.

"Yeah, and then Canada and Mexico too, when I get my passport."

"Dude, you've been saying that since high school. 'Aw man, when I graduate I'm just going to take the party van and go, man. I'll just spend five years on the road,'" said Gunshow.

"Well, one day I'm going to do it. I have the money already I—"

Phishy's back door slammed open, and a fist bumping Phishy danced into the back yard. At some point he suck back into the house. In his not bumping hand was a radio that blasted the latest indie dance music. The problem was we were all chilling and were not in the mood for his tinny, scratchy stereo.

"IT'S THE FUCKING WEEKEND TIME TO PARTY!" he yelled.

"We will party later," said God.

"NO, IT'S GO TIME! THIS IS THE KNEW H4TRICK! THE NEW H4TRICK, GUYS! FUCKING LIFTOFF!"

He boogied over to Dan and lifted him out of his seat. Then he whipped the chair into the darkness, disenfranchising Dan from comfort.

"MOVE, LARD-ASS! BURN THAT BEER OFF!"

Dan moved a little, but wasn't drunk enough for his impeccable Thriller dance.

"Dude, did you use it already?" asked Jerry.

"JUST TWO BUMPS! TWO BUMPS!"

"Wow, I gave you that like two hours ago."

God got out of her seat and marched over to Phishy. She held out her hand for the stereo but he ignored her. After a scoff and glare, she reached to take it out of his hands.

"No, no! It's fucking jam time! JAM! TIME! Fuck, fuck, fine."

Instead of giving it up, he whipped it away into the darkness of the backyard, which fortunately stopped the music. We all looked at him, waiting for the beast to make the situation more awkward. Instead he stood there, looking for something to take out his frustration on. Dan broke eye contact with him and looked at the ground. Phishy found his target.

"Dan, shouldn't you be flying fighter jets right now?"

Dan looked up, fear and pain widening in his eyes.

Phishy walked over to him. "Strange, when you graduated I remembered the dean say that you were joining the air force. For a while I didn't see you at Jerry's house. Must have been like, two years, right?"

"Yeah," whimpered Dan.

"So you *did* join the air force and fly planes, didn't you?"

"Yes."

"Isn't that fucking funny? Learned to fly a plane before you learned to drive a car! How old are you, 22? And still don't have a license?"

"Tw-twenty th-three."

"Phishy, leave Dan alone," declared God.

"It's strange though, usually guys come back with this sense of community for the armed forces. Stories, clothes, tattoos…but you never said anything about your experience. You talk all about your anime or high school, but not one peep about the military. I wonder why."

Dan looked Phishy right in the eyes; his hands and mouth were trembling. Whatever he could say was being blocked by the *run now* function firing like mad within his brain.

"It's because you got too fat isn't it? Your fucking gut would block that little steering stick and your cholesterol veins would choke you in the sky. I know it's true! You weren't this fat in high school." Phishy pushed him to the ground. The darkness hid most of Dan's tears.

"PHISHY, STOP!" yelled God.

"ADMIT IT, YOU FAT FUCK! YOU RUINED YOUR OWN FUCKING LIFE BECAUSE YOU COULDN'T STOP EATING FUCKING DOUGHNUTS! THEN THE AIR FORCE WANTED YOU AS LITTLE AS EVERYONE ELSE!

69

NOW YOU'RE BACK IN YOUR FUCKING ROOM FOR THE REST OF YOUR LIFE!"

Then Gunshow dropped his rum and jumped out of his chair. He walked up to Phishy and stared him down, all 6-feet 6-inches and 400 pounds of him. "Time to calm down, Phishy. If you're going to start shit, you're going to have to start it with me!" said Gunshow.

Phishy jumped down and started doing push-ups, the "tough guy" ones where he clapped in between. Gunshow was clearly confused by this, and normally would begin roaring with laughter. However, there were available females so he maintained composure.

"Get up, shit-head. If you want to show how strong you are, why don't you punch me so I can break your fucking skull?"

Phishy jumped up and began to jog in place. "Whatever, you guys are lame. I'm going for a run."

He jogged out of the backyard, and didn't return until hours later when we were all blackout drunk.

Gunshow picked up his jug and sat down, letting everyone absorb how well he handled the situation. This was a new moment for him, before he would have belted off some corny joke and laugh until he sat down. Somehow Gunshow learned something today; something called subtlety.

Stuck Up, 24th

Canterbury Hills was a town just south of Aberdeen. It was a small town full of big egos. There were neighborhoods of well-preserved Victorians, three story McMansions, pseudo-rustic pseudo-Villas, and turn of the millennia corporate mansions. The downtown was full of designer boutiques, lawyers, non-chain restaurants, doctor's offices, gourmet pet supply stores, investment firms, and ornate dog parks. A lot of places had these kinds of yuppie shops for their new money clientele, but in Canterbury Hills, they took their 2,000 thread count culture and waved it around to the point of satirical levels.

"Another one of these fucked up intersections!" yelled Gunshow.

"Just drive around it, but don't forget you're driving *my* car," I said.

"Well watch out," said Laura. "Cops hang out on the side of the road and ticket people when they do that."

"Fuck Canterbury Hills and their stupid traffic shit! We are driving down a fucking country road! With no fucking other cars, businesses, street side houses, and shit! Why the fuck do they have a no left turn lane?" Gunshow beat the steering wheel gently with his palm.

"Yeah, it's pretty shitty. I'm sorry, Gunshow," replied Laura.

"It's so the poor people stay out," I said. "The left turn here allows easy access of Canterbury from the filthy middle class of Aberdeen and Kirkman. And God forbid potentially one of the minorities from Victoria. The very same people that actually do any work in Canterbury."

"Fuck those rich mother-fuckers and their Goddamn Xanax wives and their shithead cocaine children! I'm gunna shoot all those fucking 1%ers in the fucking dick if they think they can exclude me! Eat shit, you narcissistic asshats!" He said while bobbing his head in anger.

"Gunshow, calm down. We're driving Megan and Laura home! Ya'know, two natives of Canterbury Hills, maybe think before you insult their people?" I said.

Gunshow brushed down his mow hawk like it could ever be in any position but down. "Shit. Sorry, ladies. You're all right. Just this damn cement triangle pisses me off. But I'll go around it. I hope there are no cops, for their sake."

"We understand. That thing pisses me off too," said Laura apologetically.

"You used this road a lot, Laura?" asked Megan curiously.

"Yeah, to see my other friends," Laura replied.

"Other friends?" asked Megan.

"Yeah, I have way more friends than these guys. You know that."

"I didn't know. We don't really talk much anymore."

"Yeah, well, my room is still across from yours." Laura turned her head to look out the window but Megan continued to stare at her. Eventually she too turned her eyes back on the road.

After the successful maneuvering known as the 12 point turn, we entered the River Walk, which was a series of parks hugging the Aberdeen River. Surrounding that were shops, restaurants, and "culture" like old movie theaters and small play theaters. The architecture tried to have some charm with colonial and European influences. However, everything was too new and too clean, so the whole area gave off a creepy movie set/dollhouse vibe. It didn't help with dozens of clustered power-moms in matching $1000 workout outfits power walking around lock in step with matching strollers.

The shops themselves were almost unique due to their store owners, but a look around the town showed that someone else had the same store idea as well. Usually an entrepreneurial power-mom would get some of her wine friends and start a business based on whatever manufactured taste she considered her own. This cupcake shop has dog cupcakes! This boutique has gypsy inspired clothing! This place has artisan cat litter!

"So are you guys heading back to Phishy's after this?" asked Laura.

"Yeah, maybe," answered Gunshow. "I'm kind of sick of that shit. I'd rather chill at home and play *Helltown 2*. Want to get online with me tonight, Ammo?"

"Sorry, man. I got work," I replied.

"What? The place closes in like four hours. What sift are you filling in? Stock counts?"

I should have continued the lie about the promotion at the grocery store, but some stupid part of me wanted to just come out with it. It would have been so easy for me to say I was filling in for someone and Gunshow wouldn't care at all.

"N-no."

"Then what are you *doing*?" His voice dripped with acid. Although his eyes were on the road, somehow he was staring at me.

"Managing." My voice dripped tears.

"We have no part-time managers."

"I know."

Gunshow shifted in his seat to prepare his statement. "So that's what Raj told you. I'm surprised he gave you the shifts so soon."

"Well, he needed me sooner than he thought." I sunk in my seat like the guilty child I was.

I could see Gunshow about to fire off, but for a rare moment in his life he held his tongue. I waited a bit for the conversation to continue but he was really holding back. I turned to looking out the window. I wondered what the sisters thought of this.

The town's constant forcing of history and importance only highlighted just how irrelevant the town actually was. Around the park paths were fancy stone light poles with little fact flags hanging off them. They usually said something like "Lincoln slept here once," "This rare bird can be found here just like the rest of the Aberdeen Valley," and "A farmer grew strawberries here."

The welcome sign to the town had a coat of arms, with a child-like craftsmanship of a field, a strawberry, three dudes, and a harlequin. The sign also attempted the rustic look, but the newness of the weathered wood made it look like it was assembled by a drunken man. The actual founding date was 1978, and was 160 years younger than the neighboring blue collar city of Aberdeen. To hide this shameful fact, Canterbury Hills only showed it in one hard to find place: the ornate-yet-still-colonial town hall.

"Hey, that's my work! Chinook Sheik! Could you take me over there, Gunshow? I need to pick up my check," said Laura.

"Yeah, no problem."

We pulled into the strip mall parking lot. It was full of women's clothing stores and niche markets. Laura's place was a high end dog food and accessories store. The front door had a no dogs allowed sign.

The inside was set up like a shoe boutique with a dozen dog friendly hand bags on one side and a dozen overpriced dog bowls on the other. There were two large circular objects filled with dog clothes in the middle. They looked like giant dark green ottomans with cubby holes around the sides. The whole place was very uncluttered, like adult swim at the pool.

Laura and Gunshow went to the counter, then into the back room. Megan and I stayed in the front to look at the dog accessories. She hugged her body like it was far too cold, but she was wearing appropriate attire. This was the first time I'd noticed her in different clothing. Friday she wore a black pencil dress, Saturday she wore a black tank top with black yoga pants, and today she wore the same yoga pants with a dark grey hoodie. There was some writing on the hoodie but I couldn't make it out; perfect conversation starter.

"So what does your hoodie say?"

She turned around from staring at the embroidered dog bowls. "Oh, it says St. Mark's gymnastics club. I was in gymnastics in grade school and middle school." She stretched it out with her hands to better look at the old decal.

"How come you didn't participate in it when you went to Victoria-Aberdeen High?"

She readjusted the hoddie back into a normal position. "They didn't have one. But that's okay because I didn't want to be in it anyway. I got to, uh…I grew out of it."

She wasn't fat, just that her breasts and hips got too large for the typical minimalist proportions of a gymnastic athlete. I would have acknowledged this, but being some sort of Christian, I bet she would have been more comfortable talking about being fat with a boy.

"Well, forget them. You earned yourself more free time in high school—something teenagers never seem to have enough of."

Megan loosened up a bit and stepped closer to me. "Heh, that's funny. I've never thought about that before. And I did use it wisely; I used that to join the debate team."

I curiously raised my brow. I couldn't believe Megan would ever talk strongly about anything. "You were in debate?"

"Yeah, that's where I met Sophia. I didn't want to but my dad made me join. He thought it would look good for college. And I think it did, I got into Rutgers University using a speech from it."

"Wow, isn't that out of state?"

"Yeah, it's in New Jersey."

"Uh oh, New Jersey. Actually, I wouldn't even know. I've only ever been to Illinois and Wisconsin. And I've walked around Missouri a few times."

Her arms finally dropped from the cradling position and to the almost convincingly rested at her side. "Heh, yeah. I've been to 22 states, the Bahamas, and Europe."

"Well don't tell God; I don't think she's ever been out of the Aberdeen valley. I mean, Chicago is an exotic place for her." I laughed a little to make it seem funny.

Laura politely laughed. "Well I would love to show her Rutgers or the Northside, or even Andalucía whenever she wanted. So you said you've walked around Missouri? I've actually never been there. What's it like?"

"I've only been to the Missouri State campus and this town called St. Geneviève. Missouri State University is like any other campus. Ste. Genevieve is a nice small town, everyone likes the University. Missouri has its interesting parts but it's not France or anything. I can see the Mississippi river from my dorm though."

Somehow, that genuinely excited her. "Really? You're right on the river?"

I folded my arms because now I had something interesting to tell, although I had no idea why. "The campus is on a little piece of Illinois that got cut off from the rest of the state. The river actually shifted around us."

"Don't rivers flood?"

"Yeah, I suppose, but the school has all of these flood safety zones. They take floods very seriously there. The town of Kaskaskia, which is the town the university is in, had some real bad floods in the 90's. If the college wasn't there it would have probably been abandoned."

"Interesting." She shoved her arms into the front pockets of the hoodie. Her eyes shifted down to the ground and then back up to me. It wasn't until this point that she made genuine eye contact with me.

"The whole area is half in Illinois and half out," I continued "At least that's how we view it."

Her eyes left mine and gazed into the hallway to the back of the store. I had to rekindle the situation.

"So have you ever been to this store before?" I asked.

She stopped looking at the back and calmly walked around the store. "No, I didn't know where Laura worked. We're not very close anymore. She got into boys and didn't want to play with me anymore."

I followed her around as she picked up the handcrafted dog clothes. "Aren't you older than her?" I finally asked.

She picked up then set down a tiny argyle sweater then looked at me. "Yes."

She didn't understand why I asked that, but that was most likely a good thing. Her soft brown eyes once again stared deep into me. I knew she was making some sort of judgment, and with her mouth assuming a very small smile, I knew it was positive.

I liked her, and I think she liked me, so I decided to ask out the girl I knew was going to be gone in August. I hoped she would be interested, but she did see me "drink" out of a toilet while probably smelling like the worst thing ever. However, those soft brown eyes told me to go for it anyway.

"So, Megan."

"Yes, Brian?"

"Would you like to do something together sometime? Maybe see a movie or get something to eat?" I held out my arms like it was a joke or something. To make it seem more honest I shrugged my shoulders and gave an open smile.

Her eyes shot wide and she took two steps back. She would have screamed if she didn't carefully think about every word that came out of her mouth. "L-Like on a d-date?"

"Well, yeah."

She began to viciously fidget with her hoodie drawstrings. I bet she was glad her shirt was very dark. "Um, uh, um, well uh, we're uh, going to be uh, very far apart in a few m-m-months."

I stepped closer to her but that just made her shake. So I took a few step s back to talk. "I think that could be a good thing. We can try out our relationship, with a convenient milestone to judge whether we should pursue it or not. It'll be easy. I'm sure you come home a lot and I'm only a train ride away from here."

"Uh..."

She rubbed her hands and stared out the window, pleading with the parking lot for an answer. Maybe I misjudged her, and her eyes were merely pretty.

"Hey, Megan. It's okay. I just think you're pretty and all…"

"Sure!" she yelled.

"What?" I was more shocked than she was.

"Sure. Let's be boyfriend-girlfriend," she said to the walls around me.

"Well let's see after a few dates to decide on being boyfriend-girlfriend."

She slapped the front of her head a bit too hard and looked at me. "Oh, uh, yeah. That's what I meant. We are uh, together then?"

"Yes. We are officially dating."

Megan held out her hand to shake like we made some business deal. I shook it because I didn't know what to do now either. She walked up to the register and put her hands on the counter, to signify that she was done with the situation. I walked up behind her to join her in staring at the back.

"And then I was like I don't care, I'll beat the deer with his own damn horn. The idiot shouldn't have gotten stuck in my tent!"

"Wow, Gunshow. That's so funny!"

Gunshow and Laura walked out laughing while the little preppy girl walked behind them, utterly disgusted. They walked right past us, still enthralled in each other. We followed behind back into the car. Laura replaced me as shotgun so I sat in the back with Megan. We left the river walk and into Canterbury Hills proper.

Gunshow and Laura were talking up a storm, which left us to sit silently alone next to each other. I didn't know what to do so I stared out of the window. Megan did the same, until we were about five minutes from her house, then she reached out and grabbed my hand. For the remainder of the voyage we looked out of our respective windows while holding hands.

The Foster's home was in the typical neighborhood of Canterbury Hills, with its rustic streets and hodgepodge of random expensive houses. The streets had old black metal lamps with more of those stupid fact flags. At the intersections were ornate street signs that said roads like "Montreal lane," "New York Blvd," and "Napa Valley Rd." The Foster's in particular lived on Lake Shore Drive.

Their house was a three-story box of plastic siding. With ten thousand windows, a four car garage, a deck that goes up to the second story, and an above ground pool to tie it all together. Everything else could just be assumed to also be overly indulgent middle class, nice lawn with lots of flowers and shrubbery, trees with bird and sunflower ornaments around them, and a heated cobblestone driveway.

"Thank you for dropping us off," said Laura.

"No problem, ladies. I hope you have a good rest of the day," said Gunshow like he was in a PSA.

"So you'll call me then?" asked Megan.

"Of course," I said.

They went in and we waited to leave like gentlemen. We drove forward a bit before I leaned up to the front of the car so I could talk to Gunshow.

"So you and Laura are clicking together pretty well, which is good timing because I just asked out Megan at the dog store."

"Fuck you, man. I mean, you didn't need to quit, just don't fucking lie to me," Gunshow said as he kept his eyes on the road.

"What? Oh, the job thing? Well shit, man, I'm sorry. Next time I lie you can hit me right in the stomach so I feel what you feel."

"I'd rather hit your face, so everyone can see what I see."

"Alright, dude. Yeah, I lied, but you're kind of overreacting about this. You can't blame me for choosing a responsible decision while not wanting to piss off my friend right away."

"Whatever, dickhead. This is your last summer and you want to spend half of it at a fucking grocery store? If I were you I'd be fucking every chick, smoking so much weed, trying new shit, and going on a fucking trip. Shit, man. You're just going to move to some fucking place and work after college anyway."

"I don't know if I'm going to move away."

"You're an engineer or some shit. We don't need a lot of those in the valley."

"Well they need a lot in Chicago; I can drive or take the train."

Gunshow gripped the steering wheel like an angry ape. "Doesn't matter; you've been fucking drifting away for fucking years. You fucking show up like twice a year. Fuck, you didn't even drop by winter *or* spring break."

I leaned forward as much as I could. "I was on trips, man. And besides, we're adults now. Adults don't hang out every night on the internet."

"Fuck, man. You and Pete were my best fucking friends. I would've taken a bullet for you motherfuckers. Hell, I'd still fucking do it. But now he left, and you're fucking leaving. Who the fuck do I have left? Fucking God and Phishy? The ballbusters? Or those other dickheads like Jerry?"

I fell back in my seat. "We've all got to move on. I'm sorry, Gunshow."

Gunshow let out a deep sigh and leaned his face against the steering wheel. He actually waited a few seconds to speak again.

"Fuck you. And fuck, I'm not moving on. No job, no girl, no school. No fucking anything."

I leaned forward again. "You'll get that shit. Don't worry about it."

"Nah, I've been the same since high school. I still got that same fucking muscles, Mohawk, and mentality. Nothing's changed. Nothing's changed."

I leaned back into my seat. "Then do something if you want to so bad. Go and fucking accomplish something. Check something off your list."

As I spoke I felt that Gunshow was finally seeing what I've been seeing for years now: stagnation. What surprised me was how he felt so far behind everyone else. Compared to my other friends, he wasn't any better off than they were.

"I fucking can't, man. I fucking can't. I just don't fucking have it. I'm just locked in some Goddamn cage and I can't even see the fucking bars. Something beyond my own fucking comprehension has a stranglehold on my own abilities and I can't achieve my own goddam goals. I'm petrified and I can't even fucking understand why."

Dragged, June 4th

Megan and I walked along the path, absorbing the nature. It was a bright summer afternoon and the sun illuminated each and every leaf, giving them a near mystical glow. Even the grass and ferns emitted a joyful hue from what sunlight they were provided. Aside from the grey asphalt walkway, the area seemed fictional; like someone used the brightest green paint and dumped it on the canvas. The air smelled fresh and earthy with all of the pheromones and pollen flowing like dancers performing the gentlest waltz. Although the air should have held heavy from how dense the young forest grew, a subtle but determined breeze kept the humidity flowing. Sounds surrounded us, yet kept their distance, like a far off city of birds, leaves, and streams.

We came upon the first landmark of the wooded path. To our left was the old silo that was used to house the harvest back when the land we walked upon was a farm.

The silo was painted with all of the history of the Aberdeen Valley. There was the first Secret Service guy who saved Lincoln from an assassin while ahistorically holding an Aberdeen flag. There were outlined water mills and smoke stacks fueling little painted factories. JFK gave his last speech in Victoria before he went to Houston, his eyes dark from either the allusion to his most famous situation, or the fact that the artist was a middle-schooler and lacked the talent to paint eyes. Apollo 12 lifted off with signature Clatcher ball bearings and knobs. Farms grew yellow globs for the first Scottish and German settlers as they erected barns and railroads. And finally, William Graham stood on his burning balcony, shouting as a slowly chipping mob yelled back.

There were no racecars, no dog pile, no homeless people and crack pipes painted on the silo. The silo acknowledged everything about the valley but made no mention of the very place it stood on: Drag Woods.

Drag Woods was once Victoria Speedway, another cultural feather in the hat for a town that could never slow down. It was built in the 1950's for a growing market of people fleeing the city for a slice of suburbia, but still wanted something to do besides mow the lawn and flirt with the milkman. It was a devil of a course, twists and turns using angles with a degree that could boil water. The maliciousness was unnecessary, for it snaked around nothing but gentle hills and a few trees. She was just the brainchild of either an evil man, or one that knew how to sell tickets. And the track did, for people all over traveled for a show of athlete against athlete, machine against machine, adrenalin against logic, and occasionally machine against pavement.

The crashes were quite the spectacle, and some even got the show cancelled for the day. But it was one in particular that closed the park for good. It was 1974 and it was another race with a dwindling, but still sustainable crowd ready for some action. The details about the racers and some junk about rivalries or whatever spiced it up, but it was an ordinary race on an ordinary day. The racers were neck and neck, surviving turns that could kink a hose, passing each other up for dangerous bravado. They were reaching the tunnel, a point that was way too narrow.

Something to know, this was the in between period of when children were considered free to ruin their own lives and when children must be protected from everything. Especially themselves.

So some kids snuck away from their parents to smoke weed, and they found behind the tunnel was the smartest place. They even had some brainpower left to dance along the tracks, pretending to be hippies or something. Of course the cars showed up; it wasn't every day you can see so many IQ points in one place. The cars got nervous and crashed into each other, but not before decorating the walls with young genius blood.

"So then they all crashed?" asked Megan

"Wh—yes, the cars crashed, blocked the tunnel and shut down the park for good."

"That's horrible." Her eyes scanned the horizon of the forest. There was no depravity to be seen, so she must have been looking for ghosts.

I held up my chest and shoulders like a tough guy. If any ghosts showed up I'd hit them. Then I'd scream and run because that obviously wouldn't work. "Yeah. After it closed this place became a haven for drug addicts and homeless people. When the gangs moved into Victoria they buried bodies here."

"Oh my! Are there bodies still here?" She got really close to me, like the situations that occurred in this place had any relevance on it now.

"No, when they found a body they would remove it. If there were any left, the animals took care of them."

"That's such a sad ending," she said, completely bummed out. "Why did you take me here?"

"Well, it's a beautiful park. In the 2000's the towns of Victoria and Aberdeen cleaned this place up. No more bums or drug addicts running around. Well, there might be some stoners chilling around here. Anyway, they also removed the tunnel, put a plaque where it used to be, then they removed all of the graffiti on the silo and guard walls, and finally repaved the track. Now it's a nice area for a relaxed date."

"Yeah, it is very beautiful. It's so bright and green," she said with cautious enthusiasm. "Are there any wrecks still around for us to explore?"

"No, they were all cleaned up. There's still some pieces lying around. But that doesn't mean there isn't anything cool to see here."

"Ooh, like what?" she said with wide eyes and a careful smile.

"Well nothing major, some old dams, an old bridge from the railroad, and deer. Sometimes you can see a fox or rabbit."

Megan once again scanned the forest, but with a pep in her step. Her eyes searched the forest floor and around the trees for critters. Animals could change her mind about anything. However they didn't seem to be around, so her interest flowed back to me. She closely examined my backpack, which obviously held surprises for her.

"What do you have in your backpack?"

Without even diverting my gaze from the path, I said, "I got a blanket, sandwiches, trail mix, apples, and candy bars. Perfect stuff for a picnic; I wonder why I brought it."

She laughed a little. "Oh how cute. But I'm looking around and the forest seems too thick. I don't see a nice area for us to sit."

"The forest is only one part. There's hills and valleys carved out from the glaciers. There's baby forests that are more like meadows with little oak and pine trees. Drag Woods also has streams and marshes. Even the Aberdeen River bumps a corner of it."

"Do they have any pictures of the drag racing?"

"No, they didn't do drag racing here. The name came from men who would dress in drag and have raves in the 90's."

"Oh." She looked down at the path in front of us. She was going to need to think through many things about this resurrected palace of nature.

I felt a vibration in my pocket. I checked my phone to see that Raj had invaded my brain space with more of his disorganized demands. Raj: You need to come in tomorrow at 5 AM. Ivanna called off so I have no opening manager. DON'T BE LATE.

I replied with a "k." The deep sigh I made was the only response I wanted to give, but Raj wouldn't be able to hear it. I joined Megan in her gaze at the path in front of us. Hopefully I could forget about this as fast as it entered my brain.

We came upon the old railway bridge that connected the river. It was our first stop on the mildly entertaining tour. And from the look of anxiety on Megan's face, I was glad it was. Her fear was not unfounded however, for the bridge was 150 years old, and the last time it had any maintenance was in the 1960's.

The thick, large planks were spaced too far apart for normal human walking, so a person had to sideways mountain climb across to traverse this mossy relic of the industrial revolution. It had two lattices, but time smashed one of them into the river, creating an artificial island of solid wooden beams beside the rotting trunks that held up the history. Sprouts sprang up from the crumbling wood and birds nested in pockets they couldn't reach. Altogether this anachronism of squishy wood posed a challenge to anyone brave enough to bring a date.

The first obstacle was actually climbing on top of it; the bridge was not at foot height but around four feet off the ground. I supposed the ground must have sunk over time. I had to give a running start in order to mount the bridge. My hands and knees were filthy from what appeared to be the process of wood turning into dirt. I held my hand out to Megan but she preferred to hug herself safe.

"Come on," I said. "This will be fun."

"No, I think it's too unsafe." She looked away into the much safer forest. Her arms were still hugging her like a straight jacket.

"I know it looks bad but I've done this a million times. Watch your step and you'll be okay."

"Thank you but I would like to watch my step from here."

"I have a really nice place for us to eat at and I don't know how to get to it otherwise."

"I don't think I should be scared on a date."

"Hey, it's alright. I've got you. Just take one step at a time."

"I lack the nerve to take one step at a time."

Megan grabbed my hand anyway and I pulled her up. She was lighter than I thought. I held her waist and she held her arms out in a t-pose as we slowly walked across the bridge. Occasionally, some loose dirt fell off the planks and she would give a little whimper, but every step she trusted me more.

"This is how people die. Not from sky diving—they have a thousand safety procedures. Not from sports because they have a medic there. No, it's people being alone and foolish for no reason," said Megan.

"That's true, but usually alcohol is involved."

"Yes. Please tell me you didn't pack any drugs or beer." She said with an extra ounce of nervousness.

"No, I don't do that stuff unless I'm hanging out with friends. When you're alone is when it's a problem." I loosened my grip on her and she continued her tightrope-style walk.

"Thank you. Do you do the hard drugs like Phishy and Jerry?"

"I've tried some party drugs like X and Molly and stuff. Never cocaine." I lifted my hands off of her and held them a few inches away from her body. She didn't move without them so I put my hands back on her.

"Why do you and your friends do those things?"

"For fun mostly, loosens us up and provides an awesome experience."

"But it seems like your group would enjoy yourselves better without them."

I had to pause and think about that for a moment. "Sometimes, yeah. I myself am starting to lose interest."

"That's good. They're all so dangerous."

"Well, you drank beer at your party."

She paused her traversing for a moment. "I did, and I regret it. I don't think I will be doing it again."

"Why did you in the first place?"

Her anxiety switched to sadness. "I wanted to feel a little more grown up. I feel like my little sister has more life experience than me."

One of the boards snapped and one of Megan's legs fell through. Her ankle was in water and a large muddy skid mark ran up her neutral gray track suit. She screamed as I pulled her back up onto the bridge. She was shaken, but also amazed. She stared at the hole for a bit before we stood back up.

The hill I wanted to show her was at the very west corner of the nature reserve, on a little sliver of land across the river. It was a steep hill; my friends and I would actually slide down it during the winter months. Blood Mountain we called it, for we'd go so fast that the snow would cut you if you touched it. I'd already told Megan enough vulgar stuff so I kept that information to myself.

When we made it to the top of the hill, I laid the blanket down on the perfect spot to see all the best views in the forest. The Aberdeen River twisted and wound through the valley; it gently pulled fishermen and kayakers as they enjoyed the summer day. Up north the river gambling boat, *Titanic Thompson* peaked just enough over the horizon to as appear half underwater. Downtown Victoria surrounded it, with Weismann tower and all of the art deco buildings keeping it swank. The hills of trees resembled fields of broccoli in the east, the silo or any identifier covered up by the massive elderly organisms. The south showed the old world charm of Aberdeen village, brick and stone shops nestled against the old trees and dormant smoke stacks of the factory district. Finally, the west had the horse ranches between Aberdeen and Kirkman. There were a dozen young horses chasing after a tractor with a bushel of hay.

"Wow, I'm so glad we came here after all," she said as she gazed at the horses.

I pulled out the items and set them next to the blanket. "This place is great. I was a little worried because I only ever come here during the winter and I was afraid the trees would cover everything up."

"This is impressive. Thank you, Brian. I really feel like this place is magical."

"You bet. Do you want to eat now?"

"No, thank you. I just want to lie down and soak in the area."

On our backs, the little pleasant moments melded together to form a surreal state of bliss. The hill was a lot quieter than the forest, only a few birds off in the distance for atmosphere. The subtle wind convinced the trees to clap their leaves for an ovation of serenity. The sun's rays casted themselves upon the grass and provided a warm temperature best enjoyed doing nothing.

The sky was full of the white fluffy clouds, the ones perfect for picking out shapes. I saw a white rabbit diving into a pool, a swordfish smashing into a pork chop, and an angel floating away. Several minutes passed since we said anything. I turned to look at Megan only to see she was fine, drifting in her own world. She seemed so comfortable on the blanket next to me, her hair emanating like a halo from a mediaeval saint.

It was a while before we said anything to each other.

"This is so nice," she said.

"Yeah, and just think, we wouldn't have this place if they didn't close it down. Thank you, foolish people. Your problems have given us such beauty."

It was silent for another wile before Megan spoke up. "Why do people do foolish things?"

"Because they don't know any better."

"But they do. So many people make such bad decisions despite understanding the consequences."

"What do you mean? Like Dan and his drinking problem?"

She turned to face me but I continued to look at the sky. "Yes. Why do we choose to make things harder for ourselves?"

"Because we're emotional creatures trapped in a logical world. We can comprehend the consequences but we can't understand them. The future has no meaning because it doesn't exist. We're monkeys with a forethought problem."

She began to fiddle with the fabric from the blanket. "That's sad. We are designed to fail and ruin our lives and the lives of others. Our mistakes burden us until we can't walk anymore."

I turned to face her. "I don't think problems are so bad. They make us who we are."

She stopped fidgeting and looked deep into my eyes. "I don't see what you mean."

I turned back to look up. "Well, a sky is only truly beautiful when there are a few clouds in it. Without a cloud, the sky is nothing more than an abyssal sea with no depth, character, or interest. The moments of sadness, pain, anger, and stupidity are what truly define us. While the beauty, happiness, and immersion are what holds us together. Everything wrong in our lives, everything wrong with ourselves, is what motivates us to be who we are."

Dan on Thoughts, June 9th

"Hey, Ammo, did you see Dan's poem?" Will asked. "I uploaded it, but I didn't see you check it out."

"What Dan? *Our* Dan? Dan Harper?" I replied.

"Yeah, when I went to pick him up yesterday I saw it up on his computer. When he left his room I copied it."

"Ha! Is it about manga?"

"No. Here, I'll show you."

"Ok, but I don't know what Dan would ever rhyme about."

Wandering back into the chasm, I see carvings of now hollow meaning.
Distilled shepherds hold their crooks with a vacant smile, satisfaction on hold
To bring forth some increments of prosperity without undermining their
Own volition towards a day of opportunistic instability.

What faculties remain are ostracized in favor of descending these ashen lands.
The eternal homelessness that is the under terrified mind is held at arm's length
Because of an understanding that this eclipse is a temporary spectacle
Instead of a perpetual night filled with callous kindness that safeguards an embarrassing fear.

I am not alone in this virtuous cycle of powerlessness escapism.

Countless members since stone was plasma held their confederation of synapses
In a jar and rattled them until the giant individuals could feel small and unified

Into a cohesive paradox that can be mitigated into a delta of
coincidental near- and mis-happenings.

Some pay a diminishing tithe of love until they are the strongest
oak,
With no observable option but to be struck by lightning.
An army of Zueses packaged inside of anagrams hold ready to
circumvent all chemical experiences.

Rocks chip and crumble upon my soul,
Reminding me of echoes filled with caution.
But I have become disenfranchised within my own vessel,
Any quagmires shall be reserved for a period after desire.

I reached the final phase of this ostracized spelunking.
My reward is the entropy of conciseness, truncated into small
clear ponds.
DNA unravels when exposed to the nostalgia of old
arrangements.

It is not until I drink the last pool that I am reminded of how far
I fell.
Like all before me I wonder why this chasm, and not the
scorched earth above it.
I hand myself a blanket and convince the ego in the ivory tower,
"Look around that plane, and tell me which direction should I
go."

Beneath the Rain, July 1ˢᵗ

The garage door was open, and it exposed an unstoppable downpour. The rain was so aggressive, so dense, that the water formed an observable membrane between the shelter and the outside that we should have been enjoying. We were all standing around the cold wet garage in our bathing suits because no one expected this violent act of nature to occur during our pool party.

"I don't know, man. This rain is only getting worse," said Phishy as he held out his toe against the current.

"Fuck that," said the Gunshow. "I'm not going to spend the whole party in my goddamn swim trunks and not swim. I even stashed some booze throughout the yard for when I get thirsty. Do you have any idea how much time I would have wasted? Naw, I'm fucking swimming."

"Wait, babe. What did you do? Where is it all? If my dad finds any alcohol he will kill me!" said Laura, utterly mortified.

Gunshow folded his arms and looked sternly at Laura. "Relax, I left a note of all the dead drops on the bench."

"The one outside? The one getting rained on?" said Phishy, almost laughing.

"Shit, I didn't think about that." Gunshow stormed out of the garage and ran through the water wall.

"Babe, be careful; it's muddy!" said Laura.

"Ah ha ha ha ha!" crackled Phishy.

The mood must have passed for Phishy as he meandered over to Jerry and Nik. Knowing them, it was something drug related; hopefully something I would enjoy.

I was standing with God and Megan, but they weren't talking about anything interesting so my mind drifted to the garage.

It was a three and a half car garage, which became a massive party zone after we moved out the cars. There were a lot of standard things like rakes, hoses, tools, and a riding lawnmower. A workbench in the corner seemed too well maintained to have ever had any use. There also weren't any signs on the wall, which reinforced the seldom used assumption.

It was easy to tell what kind of children grew up here. Pink bikes of various sizes hung from the ceiling. Dollhouses were stacked in the corner. An old freezer with butterflies and rainbows leaked as it kept our alcohol cold. Containers of Wizzney dvds lined the shelves.

To prevent any chance of parental discovery, every precaution was taken by Megan and Laura. The door to the house was locked, and we would need to ask permission to enter for the restroom. We were only allowed in the backyard, which also included the garage after the rain picked up. Everyone had to leave before sunrise, even if people insisted on helping the cleanup process. Also, no updates, pictures, or videos were allowed.

"Oh no. This was my idea," said Megan.

"What, really? Laura didn't convince you?" inquired God. She held her hands out in the standard shocked position.

"No, my dad had to go to Springfield for two days and I thought this would be a fun night. This gave me a reason for cleaning the pool. I haven't really used it since my graduation party."

"Well I'm sorry, Megan, but don't think it's going to be used tonight, unfortunately." God picked up her beer and took a few gulps for her long night. Her other arm held close to her stomach due to her lack of body heat. It was actually humid in the garage but it just wasn't warm enough for her.

"I know. I'm sorry everyone showed up in their swimwear only to stand in my garage. If I knew then I would have thought of something else."

"Hey, don't worry about it," I interjected. "Let's just all go into the house and…"

Megan waved her arms and got her whole body involved in the protest. "No no no no no, if my father found any evidence of this he would kill me."

"You mean he would kill *Laura*, and then ask why you let this happen," I said.

"Ha, that's probably what would happen," said God in between teeth chattering.

Just then, Phishy walked past us to the radio. It was casually playing some of his hipster tunes until he cut it. "Ladies and gentlemen, tonight's entertainment has arrived. All the way from a cartel kitchen in Mexico, the matchmaker, the grooveshaker, Madam Mollllllllllllllyyyyyyyyyyy!"

He reached into his pockets and pulled out two zip-lock bags of pills: MDMA. Gunshow jumped in front with half his body covered in mud. The rest of us funneled behind him. Well, everyone except Megan, who felt the party was about to get out of control. She grabbed my arm before I could get in line.

"Who is Molly? Is this dangerous?" she asked quickly.

"No, no, it's MDMA. A party drug, but not like cocaine or anything. We'll be fine. It's just something to get the mood going."

"What will it do to everyone? Will you lose control of yourselves?"

"Not at all. Hell, beer is more of an intoxicant."

"Well, will everyone be careful?"

"Absolutely."

"Well, okay. Just keep it cool."

I was the last to get mine, but the bag wasn't even half empty. There were over 200 capsules still in there. I didn't think we would use them all tonight. God got some shots ready for us and I couldn't say no to whatever cheap booze was on the menu. Sometimes even cheaper beer just didn't cut it.

"Oh, I don't need one," said Megan. She picked up a juice box that was on the shelf next to her.

"You're not drinking, Megan?" inquired God. She began to pour the bottle but she was shaking, which made her nervous, which made her shake more. Megan watched her with an equal amount of nervousness. Fortunately, she was a pro and didn't spill a drop.

She took a heavy drag from her juice box. "No, thank you. I got my drink. I can have fun with you guys without anything. But I encourage you guys to enjoy yourselves."

"That's sooooo sweet," said Phishy as he put on some thumpy rave music.

Megan looked at me as I was about to dump the powder into my mouth. "You don't need to do that, do you?" she asked.

"What? Well, I don't know, I uh…you said it was okay," I awkwardly squeaked out as I held the capsule above me.

"Well I think I made a mistake. Could you not do that tonight?" She held her juice box like a bible.

I brought it down but I still held it close. "But I want to. There's nothing wrong with it."

"It's a drug."

"There's nothing wrong with drugs. Well, this drug. I'm not going to go crazy, I promise."

"What about responsibility?" said Megan.

"Responsibility? We're 21! We don't deserve responsibility! We should be exploring our world and ourselves. This is a time to take chances to become what we've always wanted to become and leave our mark on the world. Responsibility would only be abused in our young, ignorant hands. We're just going to ruin everything we hold so we might as well have fun."

She looked at me with a wide mouth and furrowed brow but everyone else that heard me enjoyed my little speach. I grabbed my glass and I took my shot, followed quickly by the powder. Megan was upset so I walked to the open garage door. I didn't understand why she was being a hypocrite.

I felt the little bits of water touch my ankles, and the cold sent goose bumps down my arms. I looked out into the waterfall before me, its water rushing down like the loud static from an old TV. I reached out my hand to feel the downpour upon our situation. The chemical manipulation of my synapses made the water glide and dance upon my fingers. I felt this connection to the clouds that provided our lives with the water that sustained us. We were all connected in the tapestry of

Earth. The unbinding of the fibers would only ruin us. I love you, clouds. I love you.

Damn this was good shit. I did enjoy the rain though.

Everyone else gathered to the portal—the portal to the singing ocean. No one spoke but we all knew what we were thinking, and the air filled with an intensity only felt by combating chess champions. Phishy stuck his foot out but pulled it back in. The zeitgeist wasn't strong enough for him. God stuck her arm out and made a little dance, but it was too cold for her frail figure. Somehow I knew Pete would have already ran out there, no drugs required, but wherever he was, our quatumly entangled minds couldn't give me the same motivation.

Gunshow ran out first, if only to get the mud off, then Laura, then everyone else except for Megan. She stayed in the garage, waiting for us to come to our senses.

The storm was howling; aggressive, dangerous, alive. The rain slammed against all forms of matter in the valley with such a loud, continuous force that we could not hear anything but the rage of the sky. And as we dove into the pool, we celebrated the emotion of this rare live performance that could not come from a ticket or speaker.

This pool never experienced such a raw tribal collaboration of twelve people jumping and dancing underneath the cracking wake of thunderstorm. Waves flew off the sides like a topless washing machine of ecstasy and hit the ground, allowing hordes of raindrops to coalesce with like-minded molecules. We grabbed the heavy pool toys and bashed each other like the Neolithic hominids we were, channeling from the old corners of our brains. The lighter toys were captivated by the heavy metal of Mother Nature and soared into oblivion high above us. The sides were shaking and the deck was rocking but the bulwark held strong against our own unbridled euphoria.

The melody maintained its meaning in the form of threats shaped like lighting. Every few seconds one would pulsate across the sky to join the one solemn light that illuminated our otherwise nocturnal experience. Occasionally, a bolt contacted the earth but the compulsive gambler known as the young adult hubris lucked out again, for we maintained our existence for another evening.

Megan must have given up on our protection, as she was slowly stepping out to meet us by the pool. Her body was already soaked in the torrential downpour after a mere 30 seconds. She carefully took each step up the now rickety deck, griping the wobbly rail and continuously adjusting her drenched hair. When she reached the top, she looked down upon us—us bouncing, yelling animals that required context to prove our enjoyment.

We all chanted "come in" but I swam up to her to actually converse, even though I couldn't hear myself think.

"Isn't this storm crazy!" I think she said.

"Yeah, get in!" I said, or something.

"You guys look like you're having a lot of fun, but I don't know."

"You came out here for a reason, and it wasn't to watch us," I sort of said.

I held out my hand to her but that didn't make sense, being at foot level and all. So I reached under the deck for Gunshow's hooch stash number #9. It was his favorite tequila: Pedro Cali. I opened it up and held it out as she descended the stairs. That was kind of a dumb idea, holding an open liquor bottle on a 1000% humidity night.

Megan was startled by the giant bottle in her face, and looked at it for a few seconds before grabbing it. Those seconds seemed a lot shorter than they should have been. She grabbed the bottle and downed half of it before handing it to me. I consumed a less adventurous amount and put it on the side of the pool. It didn't last more than a second before a rogue wave knocked the bottle over the edge.

She wrapped her arms around me as I pulled her close. Megan's eyes were the brown that I saw at the dog food store; so soft and careful, so wide and affectionate. They must have never seen someone like this so close. Her hair melted, her makeup was running, and her clothes were drenched. Any magazine would have told her she was hideous, but to me she was more human, more real, more beautiful than anything I had ever seen. Although the rain was pounding us, all we could feel was the breath on our necks. We kissed, and descended to a quieter place below the surface.

Mall Mania, July 16th

Rainstorms hit the Aberdeen Valley on and off for the last few weeks. They dramatically rode in and out without warning like a manic depressive struggling to quit a drinking habit. And we as the citizens hid from the aggression and repaired the damage like a jaded spouse. Trees older than the country they stood upon were uprooted in a matter of minutes. They lined the soaked streets and muddy sidewalks that predated the state of Hawaii. Windows and roofs were smashed from violent episodes involving branches and wind. Cables hung and fences lay in the yards as collateral damage from a tenuous relationship between nature and civilization.

The humidity hung heavy around the damage as if the rain's life ended so violently that the very souls of the water refused to believe the present they were now a part of. The vapor touched metal and skin to consolidate from an unbearable miasma to an uncomfortable film only felt after a swim at the beach.

The river gathered then departed, but its compassion was strained on the increasing occupancy of the freshly fallen. The vanguard storms already overflowed the banks over docks, pathways, and marinas. Now the fresh conscripts escalated the situation to streets, parks, and backyards. There were no human fatalities, but the clouds in the sky implied that the siege was not over and might invoke an evacuation.

The real travesty throughout the latest barrages was the casualty of the most necessary of modern human conveniences: electricity. Sections and neighborhoods within the towns had been taken offline from the aqua guerrilla insurgents. However, the latest assault knocked the power to the whole valley. As children of the Internet, a blacked out world scared and confused us, so we traveled east, to the town of Luzern.

Luzern was a very large commercial-retail epicenter for the northwest suburbs of Chicago. Whatever could be found in shopping towns like Kirkman could be found here as well—and then some. The streaks of stucco façade buildings that emulated small main streets lined the roads. What wasn't built to be "inclusive" and "unique" were simply sprawled out strip malls with functionality chosen over design; or rather lack of attention chosen over design.

Entering from the west, one was greeted by Canton stadium, home of the Mercenaries, which was a minor league baseball team. The team was awful, and it didn't exist in the "lovable losers" category, so there were very few fans watching any games. The only time the parking lot was ever full was when the carnival showed up across the street.

Often the city government overestimated itself and believed that in a few years Luzern would be the world class city they always dreamed of.

Tall buildings went up every year, yet none of them had ever been more than a quarter full, with quarter full parking lots, and quarter full enthusiasm. Restaurants popped in and out but the walls they occupied stood near the road, waiting for the next renters to try their luck. Prairie plants slowly reclaimed the land that occupied the cement slab dividers between the roads, their ferocity increased with every yearly budget cut.

Luzern blurred the line between suburb and city wherever it could. The tall buildings could form a skyline some tourist trap would love to promote, but the distance between the semi-occupied blocks was too great to form any sort of cohesion. There were more roads than people but this did not stop the city's fun bureaucratic management division from planning cheesy carnivals and out of style jazz concerts.

Despite Luzern's screaming wiggle to relevancy, the main reason people came here were the well-designed highways from Chicago. Something the poly-ticks of Illinois jumped on with dozens of "temporary" tolls between anywhere and Chicago. Currently, it took 12 dollars from Kirkman to Lake Shore Drive.

"Jerry, your vehicle is uh, very spacious, and, uh, comfortable," said Megan, uncomfortably.

"Yeah, the party van's an awesome ride. Did I tell you that I'm going to be going across the country with this sweet momma?" Jerry replied, completely ignorant of her anxiety.

Megan didn't need to be so nervous but she had every right to be uncomfortable. This cross country explorer had seen better days since the 80's. The shag carpet and cloth seats either had a stain, crunchy spot, or cigarette burn. We were sitting on the back couch that while gave us some distance and therefore privacy from Jerry and Phishy, it also was covered in a melody of mystery stains. Her cleanliness is next to godliness brain was increasing in anxiety for every minute we were inside the vehicle. It didn't help that Jerry often spoke of his sexual and drug exploits in the party van.

"How long have you had it?" she asked as she looked into the maw of a cupholder.

He rubbed his armrest like it wasn't burned fabric at some point. "Well, my uncle had her first so I've known her my whole life. When he was stabbed to death, my old man decided to give her to me. We've been together for almost 6 years now, and she's the best ever. We're going to have an awesome time in California."

"You'd better bring me along," Phishy interjected finally.

"Well, no offence, but I only have room for someone else and uh well, yeah." Jerry rubbed his hand behind his head.

"Well what?" Phishy's thin little eyebrows curled up into a most curious form of dissatisfaction.

"Well ya'know, I would like to have that extra spot be for some ladies. Having a gay dude with me would uh, add some friction to the situation. You know what I mean?" Even from all the way in the back seat I could tell Jerry was fidgeting with his musty hoodie.

"Wow, dude. I thought you were cool." Phishy's head turned towards the window but his eyes were still fixed on Jerry.

"Hey, I'm cool with your gayness but I'm looking to score. Fifty chicks from fifty states."

Phishy turned his head back to Jerry. "What you think you're going to get, a girl every night? Do you think 'hey girl, want to get in my van?' is going to work? "

"I guess not. But I might meet just one chick that would want to come with me."

"Aren't you going to feel lonely before you find her?"

"Fine, you can come but only if you dip out when I do meet a chick. Bring a bike so you can ride back on your own."

Phishy clasped his hands and leaned towards Jerry, with eyes as almost as sarcastic as his little smile. "Kick me out on my own like that? How sweet. I wonder what you're going to do to your girlfriend when you're tired of her."

Now Jerry was beginning to get frustrated. "Well, you should be happy you're coming along at all."

"Yeah, right. Anyway, it's coming up on the left."

The crown jewel of Luzern was the Matterhorn Mall. The mall was somehow the second most visited in the country, despite the fact that so many towns nearby were trying to take a bite out of the northwest suburbs' retail economy. The leaking faucet that was Luzern's budget must have been kept afloat by this late 80's goldmine.

We travelled here as an excuse. Megan wanted to do something while her house was in darkness, and thought a date with me would be nice. Unfortunately, I was with Phishy and Jerry getting some weed and they were more than happy to interject on my plans. Well, Phishy was the one who decided he needed some game right when the power was out. Jerry came along because he was convinced to drive us.

We pulled into the parking lot and got out. Whatever isolation Megan and I had was now lost, or at least restricted to text messages. We quickly tried to make our way out of the parking lot; it appeared it was going to storm uncontrollably again at any minute.

"Hey, guys, thanks for coming with me to get the limited edition Dygobar," said Phishy. "Ieyasu only made a few thousand of them and my reservation expires tomorrow. I know you guys were expecting to do other things."

"It's okay, I guess," I said in a very unconvincing way.

This was the part I would have expected Megan to say something but her nerves must have settled back into disapproval. Jerry broke the silence.

"So what is this thing you're getting anyway? Some doll you battle online with?" he said.

"You've played Ieyasu Super Smash, right?" said Phishy.

"Yeah, I played the hell out of that when I was a kid. But I stopped when I was a kid because we are adults now—you included, Phishy." Jerry looked back at us for approval but neither me nor Megan wanted to show them any sort of acceptance.

Phishy folded his arms in disapproval. His little lips curled into a frown. "Dude, more adults play that game online than anyone else."

"Probably so they can get little boys." Jerry laughed.

"Whatever, man. You played it at my house just the other day."

Jerry put his arm around Phishy and pulled him close. Phishy's ball of curly greasy hair jiggled at the violent hug. "Yeah, I know; just like giving you shit," said Jerry.

My phone went off, so I pulled it out and silenced it before checking my messages. I didn't want them to know what we were doing. We didn't want to seem rude while they were imposing on our date. I got a text from Raj that said YOU NEED TO CLOSE TOMORROW, but I ignored the rest of the message for Megan. But I texted him back "K" before texting her.

Megan: Can we at least ditch them?

Me: That's a good idea. But we will have to be smooth about it. Just follow my cues cuz Phishy will figure us out quick.

Megan: Ok, what should I look out for?

Me: Idk yet.

Megan: Ok.

Me: Keep your txts to a minimum.

She began to type but then ended the message. Her face was shocked with self-awareness.

The inside of the mall was clearly the brainchild of a champion of some fashion that had long passed. The door handles to enter were thin, slanted, and chrome, which actually gave an accurate representation of the interior. The floor was a dark grey marble (which must have been fake, otherwise that would have been massively expensive) and had a thin gold molding. The walls were a standard white with diagonal chrome bars racing to the next store. To add some tacky flair, pink and turquoise neon lights ran parallel to them. The ceiling had skylights of little triangle windows. The geometry was arranged into rhombuses, hexagons, and trapezoids that would have cast a calm cloudy light, but instead the bright lights choked everything out.

The shops themselves contained no symmetry and instead offered little portals into wildly different aesthetics and atmospheres. They were wild and diverse; so much so that it could not make sense describing which ones were there but which ones were not. They were uniform only in the way that each one was unique, like static on a radio.

The shops each offered a point, a lifestyle, a prepackaged personality one could have by investing in the products they offered. People aspiring to become assholes or bitches went to one store, nerds into another, swimmers here, moms over there, and hippies down there. Retail was a competition for money, yes, but the stores competed through the avenue of consolidated and manufactured self-expression. What was assumed to be a mere convenience to the shopper's own agency of taste was actually a subscription to an idea of one's self, a simulacrum made real through the digestion of appealing advertisements.

"So what, the dolls play with each other?" said Jerry, clearly confused with what new gotta-have junk that was being forced down the throats of nerds and children everywhere.

"They learn from you and they fight with your moves," replied Phishy.

Jerry shook his head at Phishy and rolled up the sleeves of his hoodie. "That's stupid. Why don't you just play the game?"

"It's so you can show off your strategies," Phishy replied in complete earnest.

"Dumb," said Jerry as he gave Phishy a small push.

"You're dumb," said Phishy as he gave a push rebuttal.

Jerry pushed his shaggy blond hair back, which disgustingly stayed in place. "Just admit that you are an Ieyasu fanboy and trying to buy some collectable."

"Oh, I absolutely admit that." Phishy laughed.

We arrived at the middle of the mall, which had a lounge and a very tall, detailed, and incomprehensible map. The lounge required a few steps down some marble stairs into a pit to reach it. The floor was a break from the rest of the mall, for it had worn striped black and white carpet. The couches were replaced at some point but not soon enough. There were standard chair and loveseat sizes made out of a plastic material. They had pink arm rests, black bottom cushions, and a turquoise back. Marty McFly would have been impressed with the décor.

Stepping down into the pit to look at the map gave me a fantastic idea. The mall went in three directions at this point and it gave an organic opportunity for us to divide. I turned to Phishy to set the scene.

"So GamerGate is to the left, but I think Megan wanted to go to…Philosophy," I said. "But it looks like Philosophy is in the North wing. We can split up. I mean, you guys probably don't want to go to a girl's store, especially you—Jerry."

"No, I do not," replied Jerry. That was all of the convincing he needed.

Megan fizzled on from a sort of disappointed stupor. This was her cue, and all she needed to do was agree. Too bad Phishy winced like a cowboy before she spoke.

"Yeah? Maybe I do want to go to Philosophy, to look at stuff and do gay things. What do they sell there, Megan?" he said as he stroked the half dozen hairs below his chin.

"Uh…they, uh, um, Phil-o-so-fee-dress-es? And uh, uh, dia-pers-fum?"

Phishy and Jerry busted out laughing. I looked at her and she gave a small, apologetic face. I shook my head. Well

104

we're going to have to try really hard now. They were still laughing.

"Wow, girl. You are nuts. Ha ha, let's go to GamerGate," said Phishy as he wiped a tear from his eye.

They walked first while we followed with our tails between our legs.

Me: Philosophy dresses? Why didn't you think of anything else?

Megan: I don't know, I wasn't ready.

Me: You need to be ready cuz he's on to us now.

Megan: Why don't we just go?

Me: We can't.

Megan: Why not?

Me: You can't just do whatever. You just can't.

She looked at her phone for a while before putting it away. Instead of looking at me, her mind wandered off while her body followed us. Her white sandals kept up despite lack of communication from her head. Phishy drifted from walking with Jerry to walking aside Megan.

"Gray tank top and bleached jean shorts. Did you borrow those clothes from your sister?" asked Phishy.

"No, I have revealing clothes too. She doesn't have to be the only one to live her life however she wants," replied Megan.

Phishy held his hands up. "Hey, I'm not judging your character, just trying to get a conversation started."

She adjusted her hair and rubbed her now tired eyes. Her blank stare implied that she was beyond the displeasure of my friends ruining her date. "I'm sorry, I just get compared to my sister a lot, and she gets compared to me a lot. It's funny, my friends say I should change but my family says I'm perfect. And then my sister is told the opposite. I think it really upsets us both."

Phishy paused at the fact that she told him something so sincere. He licked his tiny mouth at the fact that he too should reply with something so sincere. "My brother is off in LA acting in commercials while I'm some bum, so I can understand. My dad's a big jock so we were both in sports

105

growing up. My brother broke half the records for every sport while I sat on the bench. So yeah, I understand sibling comparisons."

She was equally surprised at *his* sincerity but her tired face barely showed it. "I'm sorry to hear that. I don't even understand why people think I'm failing at life. I get perfect grades and I have fun even though I never partied before 21. And I actually do have friends."

"Well, if you haven't noticed, I am an asshole. But that's because I've learned that you just can't keep everyone happy. I mean, my brother is in four perfume ads. How am I supposed to compete with him?" Phishy shivered in his honesty.

"No offence, but I don't think I'm the uh, right kind of person to follow your example, Phishy. I mean, I don't think you're a bad person, I just uh…"

"Don't be me; just be yourself. Do what you want to do. Forget what other people say."

We arrived at GamerGate, the nation's monopolistily large game store for preorders and gamers, in that order. It was a small hole in the wall filled with TVs, toys, and games. Games for every console lined the walls, and the rest were in bargain bins or freestanding shelves. Walking space was limited, and it was designed with a natural flow to the cashier before exiting the store. The floor had interesting carpet that was stained by years of dropped gamer fuel and health potions. On the televisions was a guy half-interviewing half-promoting a new game and how soda pop sponsored this and how you should drink it, bro. In the corners were cardboard cutouts of linebackers with hand cannons and bimbos playing volleyball.

The registers had two attendants: a guy with a long greasy comb over that covered one of his eyes and a girl with 90's boy band hair and an attitude of knowing everyone at work didn't understand that she was a human being. The guy had a wrinkled collared shirt and previously nice pants with a chain wallet. The girl had tattoos of recognizable game characters on 50% of her body. She wore 50's pinup makeup and a faded t-shirt that might have said preorder today.

The line was a bit long and had participants of varying levels of hygiene, men and women included. There were children in line with a required parent to purchase a game that was less violent than the movie they saw last night. There were guys dressed nice enough to possibly convince a girl that he did not know more games than words. There were girls dressed in fall weather clothes giggling about anime characters; some were anorexic and some were obese. As I looked past them, the largest type of person was normal.

We got in line and Jerry ran off to talk to the anorexic weeaboo girls (little did he know they stalked for life). Phishy didn't look at any of the games because he, like 95% of the customers that entered this store, already knew what he wanted. I glanced at a few games on the wall while Megan spun in this undiscovered culture.

"Hey, I know you guys want to be alone, and I'm okay with it. So you guys can head out," said Phishy as he coolly leaned against a stand of gift cards.

"Really, man?" I replied, utterly dumbfounded.

"Yeah, just meet us downstairs by the Korean place when you want to go."

"Wow, sure. We'll see you there."

Phishy shot up in defense. "Wow? What do you mean 'wow'? I'm a cool guy."

"Yeah, I know," I said apologetically.

We walked out and hung a quick right back into the badly lit mall. Although the ac was a bit too cool, the lights shined a feeling of a hot dry day.

"So where do you want to go?" I asked.

"I'm not sure," said Megan.

She looked over to the stairs we were passing and followed it with her eyes. I thought she was going to lead us down there, but she moved her head foreword. It seemed like I was going to decide the fun.

I did decide—or at least I tried to. We stopped at fancy food places and tried the free samples of various teas, cakes, meats, and cheeses. There were technology stores with electronics for us to play games or to simply fool around with.

We changed the wallpapers of each tablet and computer to Dan doing his drunken thriller dance. The novelty and niche fashion stores held tons of goofy clothes for us to mock and mess with. Occasionally, we sat on the squiggly line benches and people-watched the thousands of human beings walking the mall.

We sat at a bench that overlooked the bottom two floors of the mall. It was at the center of the mall, and the glass railings allowed us to see the shoppers clearly. Two stairs circled each other around the hole and offered a design-friendly way to descend the building.

We were having fun, but I could tell that there was a film over her, some sort of filter that was occupying her mind and letting only the smallest amount of pleasure through. I tried to get her out of it. I attempted to talk about the current situation, or just things that in the end were meaningless. Everything I tried didn't work and I just decided to prod at what was bothering her.

"So why are you so bummed out, Megan?"

She leaned back against the chair and stared at the ground. "Nothing, just not feeling well."

"Was it the stinky cheese?" I jokingly replied.

"Ha, no I'm just not into it."

"Why? We're finally doing what we want. Are you still mad about Phishy?"

She gave a deep sigh. "No, it's my own fault."

Now I didn't know what the hell was going on. "What is it?"

"In high school I would roam the hallways alone during the mornings and lunches. I wanted to look too busy for everyone. I didn't feel comfortable being around anyone, even with people I knew very well. People would say hi to me as I passed and I would say hello. If I was feeling less vulnerable I might talk to them. I would always leave though; can never get too close or I'll be burned. I remember your clique, always having such a good time with your crazy events. Like when you guys tried to crowd surf Phishy to class or get Dan as homecoming king."

"Wow, yeah. Dan actually won; he still wears the crown if you ask him to bring it. I remember when I would jump out of garbage cans and scare people or when Gunshow moved the cars in the parking lot into the shape of a penis. But why did that bother you?"

Her eyes met mine for a moment before shooting down back to the floor. "You and your friends had so much fun and there I was avoiding people for no reason. I made myself alone."

"Well, you're not alone now. You have so much to look forward to. Everyone was an idiot in high school; it's part of the package." I attempted to comfort her by putting my arm around her but it didn't seem like she even noticed.

"I still do it now. I just hide out in my dorm room between classes."

"Well, college is just high school 2.0. And you're hanging out with us."

She lifted my arm off of her and tilted her head towards me, although she still avoided eye contact. "Text Phishy. I want to go home."

"Okay."

I pulled out my phone but she already got up and walked to the stairs. She put her hand on the railing and looked down. I got up to meet her. She lifted her hand up. I looked up at her. Maybe if the air was still and ominous, maybe if I wasn't so distracted, maybe if I was quicker I would have caught her.

It should have been in slow motion. It should have had some dramatic music with one lady singing in a foreign language. The lighting should have been darker with a spotlight on her and everyone else would have been too dark to see.

Her hair should have danced so gently as her eyes closed with a noble determination. She would have worn a long black dress that would have flowed in unison with her hair to symbolize the dark yet graceful tone that shifted into the character.

She should have landed into a dark sea of release, destruction, and rebirth. As she quickly descended into the abyssal sea, the darkness would slowly drown her, to visually express the claustrophobia and hopelessness her mind imprisoned her with. Finally, her hand would slowly extend downward, to pose a question to the audience that only context and reflection could answer.

That's how it should have felt. That's what I felt she deserved. That's what would have been necessary for me to see how much of a red flag she was waving.

Instead I experienced the fastest moment of my life. She fell hard, she fell fast, and she fell loud with the glass sidings smashing from the impact of her limbs. A dozen or so flights of marble stairs took their toll on the ungraceful girl barrel rolling against them.

Casting Party, July 19th

Megan lay in the bed with both of her legs suspended in the air. Her arms were held down by a tightly wound white blanket. Stained bandages and casts were all over her body, preventing any movement. Her forehead was covered, so the only exposure was her face from the eyes down. There was also some sort of bandage in her mouth that would have prevented her from speaking. So altogether she was a mostly white mummy with very little in the way of communicating with us.

The hospital room was large, about the size of a one-bed hotel room. It was complete with a huge TV, couch in the corner, and a nightstand that had seen a lot. It also had non-motel things like the hospital equipment and a white board with writing of people that at least pretended like they wanted to be there.

However, despite the large size, it could not contain all ten of us. It was originally just going to be me, however God decided to come because Megan was technically her friend first. She asked Laura if she was going to be there. And although she already visited her, she didn't get the chance to write on her sister's cast. Even though Laura was only a few minutes from The Lamb of God hospital, she made Gunshow pick her up.

Phishy caught wind of this and invited himself along with Jerry as a driver. However, Jerry was already hanging out with Will and Dan so they came along. Nik wanted to bum some drugs off Jerry and came with too. I wasn't sure why Alex was there though.

"So is she dead?" asked Nik as he gazed directly into her eyes.

"No, you idiot. She's just asleep," I replied as I pulled him back.

Nik ignored my insult and tried to shake Megan. I grabbed his wrist to stop him.

"Nikolaos, leave her to rest! She fell down a lot of stairs and her body needs to heal," declared God.

He backed off and looked at everyone in the room judging him. We already judged him based on the other dumb things he'd done, but if he knew that he would either cry or act out harder.

"Damn, this is a nice hospital. Much nicer then Victoria General," said Gunshow.

"Well this is what happens when a hospital is in a district with lots of old rich people," I replied.

Gunshow poked the expensive television. "Damn, rich geezers did all of this?"

"Well yeah, and their rich kids. We are in Canterbury Hills," I said as I held back Nik from touching Megan again.

"Yeah, I know. I fucking drove here! Why the fuck do they block a right turn? A right fucking turn in the middle of fucking nowhere!" Gunshow kicked the little metal garbage can in frustration.

"I'm sorry my town is full of snotty rich people. I promise I'm not like that," said Laura.

"Yeah, I know, babe. You're too unique for this place," said Gunshow.

"Aw, thank you, babe!"

"Ooh, babe, babe, babe," said Phishy in a snotty, mocking voice.

"Well, I came here to sign a cast and I'm going to do it. It's what I've wanted my whole life," said Nik.

111

"Liar, I know you wanted to bum some weed off of Jerry," I said.

"Hey, not so loud," Jerry said.

"And since he said no, now you're looking for an excuse to not look like a fool," I said.

"Whatever; I'm doing this."

He leaned over with the marker in his hand, but God grabbed his wrist. "I don't think it's right. She's not awake. She doesn't know we're doing this. I think we should leave."

"Fuck no! I didn't deal with this shit to look at a sleeping chick. I'm going to write 'Get well soon' and no one's going to fucking stop me!" said Gunshow.

"Yeah, I had to drive down Kirkman road on a Saturday. I deserve something," said Jerry.

"Alright, but if she gets upset I'm blaming all of you," said God.

Nik went first; he creatively wrote out, "Get well soon." Even though he carefully wrote each letter, it still had the penmanship of a drunk toddler.

"How original," I said.

"Hey, it's what I wanted to say," he replied.

Gunshow was next; he grabbed the marker out of Nik's hand and wrote, "Fuck those stairs."

Laura wrote in the most girly font ever: "Sorry, sis. Broken bones sux."

I wrote: "I promise to carry you up every flight of stairs for now on."

Phishy wrote: "Don't read this or your leg will itch."

Jerry wrote: "Guys also dig chicks with scars."

Dan wrote: "Sorry ☹"

Will wrote: "Have a super recovery." He didn't like what he wrote, but he had nothing to say. He was swept up into this situation, and he knew he shouldn't have been a part of it.

Alex wrote something boring and unimportant.

God wrote: "This was a terrible accident and I want you to know that you are always welcome to call on me for any assistance you may need. I don't think I can lift you but if you need someone to push your wheelchair or assist in necessary stretching I am more than happy to help. I know the pain must be terrible but I know some yoga techniques tha—" I grabbed the pen out of her hand before she looked for a publisher and movie rights.

"Now she has something fun to wake up to," said Laura as she held her hands together in excitement.

"Yeah, she looks happier already," said Jerry.

"How do you know?" I asked suspiciously.

"Well, there's less of that stuff leaking out of her mouth."

"Okay, guys. We did it. Let's go home," Phishy said as he paced around by the door.

"We can't just leave yet. Maybe she'll wake up and then we could actually visit her," said God.

Phishy increased his movements. "This place bothers me. Reminds me of my first boyfriend,"

The veterans made a collective sigh. With so many people in one room, how else could Phishy resist grabbing the spotlight? Unfortunately, the newer people didn't know any better and even if his story was true, he wasn't going to be sincere about it.

"What was wrong with your first boyfriend?" asked Laura. She sat on an open corner of Megan's bed and petted one of Megan's casts.

Phishy put his hands in his pockets and leaned like a limbo contestant. It appeared like he may have not wanted to actually tell this story. "Well, his name was Christian. He was a close friend to my brother Marco. Marco broke his foot in football or basketball or hockey practice so he was here recovering. Well Christian and I visited him together. We were very close. As a matter of fact, we discovered who we really were together. We were always talking and chatting, and since he was my brother's friend it was an easy way to keep a secret."

"What happened at the hospital?" she asked.

He began to speak a lot faster. "Good question. So Christian and I really developed ourselves since we were surrounded by strangers and my brother was stuck in the bed. A nurse asked my brother about being gay since we were so open

113

about it. My brother freaked the fuck out then called my dad and Christian's dad. I got my ass beat and I never saw Christian again. Then my brother chalked up another reason why he's better than me in the eyes of my family. So yeah, I hate this place."

"Well, we're here for Megan, not you," said God.

"Obviously. I just can't take being here and she isn't going to wake up so let's just go."

He grabbed Jerry's arm and tried to pull him out the door but he refused. Then he went after God but she impolitely declined as well. After more refusals by Nik and Dan, he threw his hands up in frustration.

He stomped out with Spanish swear words flying out of his mouth. He said quite a few as he went down the hall before the nurses asked him to stop.

Ieyasu Seal of Approval, July 25th

"I'm sorry the casts are difficult to get up the stairs," said Megan.

"Well, here. I've got an idea," I replied.

I lifted her into my arms and carried her up the stairs. I was careful, for her leg casts and neck brace made her stick out, and I did not want to add any more injuries. Broken legs, fractured skull, broken wrist, damaged shoulder, a comically broken (and casted) middle finger, along with bruises and cuts on over 75% of her body was more than enough for a human being to deal with. Also, her father was home. And one little "ouch" from his daughter would send me flying out the house. I should know; he told me when he answered the door.

I used my feet as antenna to feel out every step. I muttered *Measure twice cut once* in my head.

Thank God those big box homes had wide ass stairways. Pick any 19th century bungalow from Aberdeen and it was a negotiation to get a large pizza up the stairs, much less a horizontal human.

"I hope you're not getting any flashbacks going up these stairs," I joked.

She laughed. "No, I'm okay. Just uh, don't say stairs anymore."

"Understood."

It must have taken a few hundred years to finally reach the top. I tried to reach in for a victory kiss on her busted lip but she turned away. She smiled a little, though it made me notice her missing bottom teeth. I carried her into her room and laid her down on the bed.

She sat up, which was quite a task considering she was completely covered in white casts and bandages. Although, she didn't look entirely like a cartoon mummy, because there was some pale clothing that showed through. The only real color

115

was from the notes left by me and my friends written on her casts.

"I haven't had a boy in my room since I was 11," she said.

Neither had a decorator. The wall was painted a pale blue with Wizzney princesses lining the ceiling. There was one big bay window that had stuffed animals resting on the cushy counter. The floor was a shaggy pink carpet that had dimples from when something was moved. It also had tracks from when the vacuum came through, but no footprints.

Her small bed was a pale pink with even more princesses bursting out of a pink heart. It had a powder blue trim around the side and frame to match. There was a chair by the window, an aging office throne from the sixties that had a green and brown checkered pattern fading in the sun. Opposite to the chair was a very organized, fake wood desk with shiny flowers and smiley face stickers stuck to the metal legs. The desk's chair was a grey cushion office chair with nail polish marks all over the plastic arm rests.

Next to the desk was a closet with a picture of singing cartoon cats hanging above. On the side facing the corner of the room was a framed high school diploma. Next to that was a dresser with neatly organized beauty products covering the surface and a standing mirror that was facing the wall. Next to that was a neatly organized doll house collection that must have amounted to $10,000 worth of pink plastic.

Finally was the old flat screen TV inside of an old pine entertainment center with every cabinet but two filled with Wizzney movies. One of the cabinets had pictures of her family and the other had an old Ieyasu Entertainment System.

Naturally, I ran over to the video game system. "Wow, the original Ieyasu System! Does it still work?"

"Yes, though I haven't played it in a few years," she said, half-exhausted.

I picked it up and inspected the quality. "Well, it looks like it's in perfect condition! It's not even dusty!"

She rested her head against the wall by her bed. "Do you want it? I feel bad that it's always here but I never play with it."

"Of course! What games do you have?"

With a deep sigh she said "Super Psilocybin 6, The Legend of Link, The Last Fantasy, The Flight of Michael, and a few more."

Like a kid straight out of an '89 commercial: "The Flight of Michael? I've never played that one before."

She closed her eyes and smiled. "It was my favorite game. You play as the angel Michael who has to stop Lucifer from taking over heaven. The flying obstacle tracks were my favorite part."

"So when do you want it back?" I said as I inspected the controllers.

"You can keep it," she said with her eyes closed.

"Really? I don't know; I don't want to take it from you. Especially if I'm not giving you anything for it."

She slowly reopened her eyes. "You don't need to give me anything. You've given me more than enough. Please keep it."

"Well, okay then. But whenever you come over I promise you unlimited access to it. And also, if you change your mind I will be happy to give it back."

"Thank you, Brian. You're always so nice."

I began to unhook the console when Megan's father, Mr. Foster, knocked on Laura's door, which was across the hall from Megan's.

He was tall with a shaved head. The rest of him was thin and muscular, which required a lot of discipline for a man in his fifties. His eyes weren't brown like the Foster sisters', his were an uncomfortable blue. For his eyes didn't see; they only interrogated. He also lacked the wrinkles on his face to show any history of experiencing emotions.

"Sweetie, why don't you come out of your room and be with your sister and her new friend?"

Laura opened her door angrily, and half dressed. She had her phone in her hand.

"I can't. I'm leaving. And besides, they can't do anything with Meg covered in bandages so chill out," she said with a brush off attitude.

"Young lady, I don't want to hear attitude. And who are you going with? It'd better not be with that gun guy again. He's a bad influence."

"Dad, stop. He's a really sweet guy when you get to know him. He always sticks up for people and he always takes care of me. You would like him. "

"Then I want to meet him."

"No, Dad. No. And I'm running late."

Her phone rang as she was putting on a hoodie over her shirt. She grunted as she rustled with the phone. "Dammit, babe, already? Ah, I'll be down soon just stay in the car!"

"Who's babe?" said Mr. Foster.

Laura ignored him and ran down stairs as she applied her makeup. After the door slammed, the Bulletwagon could be heard driving off in the distance.

Mr. Foster looked down the stairs for a bit before turning into Megan's room. He looked straight at her and kept careful attention to not look at me. Even though in his mind I was all he could see.

"Do you need anything, angel? I can make sandwiches or lemonade. Do you want me to order you guys a pizza? How about Chinese food? I could order your favorite, chicken and vegetables."

She looked at him and smiled, "No thank you, Father. We will be okay."

"Are you sure? Do you want root beer or some pillows? Do you want me to bring a movie up from the garage?"

"I am fine, Father. Thank you."

"Okay, angel, just call me up if you need anything. I'm always listening."

"Thank you."

Only then did he look straight at me and gave me a hard deep stare only a cop could perform. "It's nice to meet you, young man," he said in an aggressively cynical voice that thousands of actors aspired to capture on every cop show.

As he walked away, I could feel the room breathe out again. The color restored in the walls and the birds returned to chirping.

Megan rubbed her eyes with her good fingers. "That's nice the birds are back. There used to be a nest on that window. Every day I would watch the chicks grow a little bigger until they finally flew out of the nest. I miss seeing them."

"That's cool. I wouldn't expect much else to see out of this window. A quiet street lacks stimulation."

She returned her head to the side of the wall. "Well, usually I would see Laura getting picked up for parties. There would be ten or so people stuffed into a car. A bunch of them would have to get out and rearrange themselves for her to fit. Late into the night she would come home wasted. She usually had a few friends sit with her on the lawn and hang out until she sobered up. They would be joking and laughing. Sometimes I would see her make out."

"How long were they out there? It should have been a while before she was cool."

She closed her eyes again. "They had a ritual. They would hang out until they had to puke then they would crawl over to our neighbor's bushes, and uh, it was disgusting."

"Nasty."

"Yes, they named the bush puke plant. They would shout it out when somebody barfed."

"And nobody heard? Not even your father?"

"These houses were made soundproof because of the planes from O'Hare, and the air conditioning is sort of loud."

"Add in that all the houses are the same and you have one oblivious neighborhood."

"Yes."

"But your dad didn't have any suspicions? He's the sheriff of Aberdeen County. I'd expect him to have two squad cars on her at all times."

"Daddy just refuses to believe we can be capable of such hedonism. And she takes advantage of him."

"You call him Daddy?"

"I used to until I got made fun of at volleyball practice."

"When were you in volleyball?"

"Last year."

"So where's Mommy?" I smiled, hoping she would get the joke.

She didn't, and everything was silent for what was quickly becoming forever. "She's gone. When I was a little girl she told my dad she was a homosexual. She only had children with him because God told her to and she actually didn't love him. My father didn't want us to be exposed to her and kicked her out. He removed every picture and erased her from our lives. When we asked, he said she abandoned us and God for selfish desires. I never heard from her again."

"Wow, that's horrible. Do you think she's tried to contact you?"

Her voice began to slur as her drowsiness increased. "Laura is convinced she's tried. For years she would sneak around, digging through the mail and checking the messages for her. She got in touch with my mother's family but they cut her off too. If she has then I don't think it's possible without showing up at our house."

"Where do you think she is?"

"Well, one night my father was drunk and muttered something like 'Ran away to Holland to be with the dykes that dike' so I think he was talking about her."

"Do you miss her?"

She opened her eyes and lifted her head off of the wall. She looked around the room for an answer. Unfortunately, nothing was written on the walls so she was forced to reopen some old wounds. "I...I don't know. When I was a child I would often play with my dog Sunday when I should have been asleep. One time I heard them yelling so we snuck over to eavesdrop. I heard her say she couldn't live this lie anymore and she would rather die than be in this marriage for another day. I heard her choose to leave us."

"I don't think she wanted to be away from you and your sister, just not with your father."

She was quiet again, and a tear formed before she spoke. "Perhaps. It's not that she was gay. Although at the time my church and family convinced me that homosexuality was her greatest sin. When I reached high school I stopped blaming that and learned it was all because she abandoned me. She left me alone to deal with my life. When I told my friends what she did they turned around and picked on me. They got the whole school to join in, calling me homo and lesbian. No girl wanted to be my friend because they thought I was going to rape them. Someone convinced my teachers and they would constantly ask me if I was actually gay. Even when I told them no they took me into special classes and showed me videos on how to be a proper lady. The principle tried to convince my father into sending me to a special camp to correct me. Thankfully, my father was the only one who believed me and let me go to public school after that."

"Wow."

Now more tears formed and her face blushed with sadness. She gave a soft, gentle cry before she spoke again. "She was never there; I prayed for her return. I begged God that even though she was gay, I still wanted to see her. I wanted my father to let her back in or for her to return to us. I needed her to fix the pain she caused. I wanted her to guide me through life like she always did."

I got up and put my arm around her shoulder. This time she acknowledged it. "I'm sorry that happened to you. Fuck those stuck up bitches and their lies. But your mom is still out there. You can find her and get some answers."

She wiped her tears on her cast. "It's too late for that. I don't care about her anymore. She didn't try to contact me so I'm not going to contact her. I would have loved her all the same and supported her unusual romances. She would have been the only one that understood that I was not gay. But whatever. I don't want to talk about her anymore." She struggled to cut off her crying.

"I'm sorry I brought her up."

"Don't be. I have a case for the game system. You should use it to carry it home."

"Oh yeah, I forgot about the IES."

I went into her closet and grabbed the case she was talking about. It was actually in excellent condition considering the fact that it was older than me. I was putting it away when Megan spoke up.

"It doesn't hurt, and it should."

I turned around. "What? Letting me borrow this?"

She gazed at her broken legs. "No, my injuries. I broke so many bones, so many cuts, yet all I feel is itchy. I should feel horrible; my body is in so much trauma."

In a very positive tone I said: "Well modern medicine, right? Besides, don't you have pain pills?"

Now she was examining the casts on her hands and arms. "Yeah, a whole bottle, but I haven't taken any. I want to feel this."

"Why?"

"You said it yourself. Pain defines us, and I need some definition."

I set down the game system and stood next to her on the bed. "Then let me define it with you."

"What?"

I climbed up onto the bed. We laid there together and watched out the window. The sky let a few raindrops hit the glass, and the sun receded behind the clouds to cast a mild, low, light.

Megan turned to me, and I saw the same soft brown eyes that captivated me. They seemed to have been the only content thing about her. "You know, I became friends with Sophia because I thought she was a lesbian. I wanted to get to know someone like that. I was surprised when she was dating that Peter Gomez."

I laughed so loud it scared her. "You have no idea how many people have told God that. It's the story of her life. We used to give her so much crap for that. Wow! I *know* you haven't told her because she would have killed you. Ha, wow, what a blast from the past. And his name is Pedro Gomez. He would say 'Peddy sounds weird so call me Pete.'"

"How long did they go out?"

122

I had to wipe the tears from my eyes. "Only a few months. It turns out being friends with someone since grade school makes it difficult to be in a relationship. I'm glad they took the high road and ended it before it got bad."

"Have you ever thought about her?" she coyly asked.

"Like that? No, I'd rather date Miyazaki, Phishy's cat."

She was about to say something but her face froze. Her brain was on fire, looking and analyzing everything. It didn't take long for her to pass judgment on her discoveries because her face sank into a sober understanding.

"You said that at my birthday party," she said robotically.

"I did? Sounds like me," I said jokingly.

"Yeah, then Gunshow demanded that you prove it. So you kept saying here, kitty kitty jokingly through the night."

"Well, even drunk I wasn't actually going to do that."

"I know, but Gunshow pants'd you and you guys were laughing, which scared Sophia. So she told you to wait in the basement as she hid the cat. And then I remember everyone laughing about how they forgot about you."

"Wow, I must have been pissed."

"So that means you were in the basement the rest of the night."

"So?" I said suspiciously.

She was about to speak but needed to think again. After a while she shook her head like 'forget about it'. We turned back to the window and watched the drizzle drift into a dense torrent.

Creak, May 23rd

Megan's gentle brown eyes stared deep into mine as I told her another one of my crazy antics with Pete from high school. Every one of her smiles, laughs, and "Wow's lifted me out of the still hung-over mindset. That was the happiest I've seen her all weekend. It was something I should have realized, despite the fact that I had no reason to be alert.

Between my tales, the honesty would leave her eyes as her gaze dropped to the car floor and then out of the passenger window. Her smile would flatline, and a shroud of instant isolation would envelop her. I would reintegrate her back into the conversations, and see that charming smile again. However, as God drove closer and closer to Phishy's house, her depression would return faster and faster. This burden choked her heart so much that no anecdote could revive it.

I wasn't yet close enough to her, so I took her reaffirmed indifference as a sign to focus more on my friends. As we turned onto Phishy's street, she practically became a ghost as I conversed with God and Will about machines.

After our debacle on Kirkman road, we returned to Phishy's house for another day of entertainment. God decided to drive us back because I was obviously fed up with driving for at least the rest of the weekend. To avoid parallel parking, God decided to park a bit down the street from the actual house. As we got out and walked over, Nik and Phishy could be heard in the distance yelling at each other in the front yard.

"Hey, man. This is so dumb. Why do we have to pick these up? I didn't drink out here," said Nik.

"Because it looks bad out here, and everyone else is asleep or out," said Phishy angrily.

Nik kicked a can. "Stupid. I should have left."

"Now you see what it takes to be a nice person," Phishy said sarcastically.

"Shut up, Phishy. I'm a nice guy! I'm in your driveway picking up bottles and cups right?"

"While complaining, I might add."

We approached Phishy and Nik picking up trash; their bags were mostly full. Phishy was in his standard band shirt and jeans while Nik was in Phishy's dad's clothes.

"Looking good," I said to Nik as I pointed to my paint-covered shorts, courtesy of Mr. Ortega.

"Yeah, I wanted to wear one of his dad's suits but he made me wear this," said Nik as he pointed to his burrito in paradise shirt and Victoria-Aberdeen High gym shorts.

"I'm not a charity. If you guys want to look good after hurling on your clothes then how about, maybe, I don't know, bringing another outfit?" Phishy rolled his eyes at his own statement.

"Well, I didn't think I'd be here all weekend. I should have left with Rick and them," said Nik as he threw a bottle in the bag like a grumpy toddler.

"Oh, Rick left?" said God. "That's too bad."

"Yeah they all left after they sobered up this morning. It's just the usual now, with the Foster girls," said Phishy.

"Oh, we're not the usual?" asked Megan.

"After this party I think you girls earned the title 'usual'," said God.

"So anyway, where did you guys go without me?" asked Phishy.

"Some Mexican restaurant on Kirkman," said Will.

"Pricks, I knew you guys wouldn't stick around and help out. I'm always the one cleaning up, I'm always buying new shit for my bed. I'm always getting yelled at by my parents…"

"We got you a burrito," said God as she handed him a burrito

"Wonderful." Phishy took off the tin-foil wrap and proceeded to eat like an animal.

The front door to Phishy's house opened and Jerry came out. He had recently woken up, as evidenced by his apprehension to the sun and half of his shaggy blond hair smushed flat. He covered his red eyes with his 'distilled' blue hoodie. The holes and stains were accentuated by the harsh summer afternoon light. His pants were ripped and his shoes were untied but no major stains; he knew his binge limit.

"Hey, did that Jackie girl leave?" Jerry asked.

"Yeah, she left with her boyfriend, Rick," said God.

"Well, she didn't mention a boyfriend when we were dancing last night. Or when we were watching the sun come up on the deck. Or when I put my hand up her shirt."

He reached into his hoddie pocket and pulled out some plastic sunglasses with one of the lenses missing. As he walked down the porch to us, he rubbed the surviving lens and put the shades on. "Ah, somewhat better," he said.

"So what do you guys want to do? Stand around and not help me clean?" said Phishy to an audience of lazy friends.

Jerry pushed back his slimy yellow hair. "Hey, God, you were looking good last night on the dance floor…"

"Well I was enjoying myself and *only* myself," she replied.

"But you were with Megan," he said.

Megan stood next to God to back her up. "We were enjoying ourselves together," she said prudishly.

Jerry put his hand behind his head and laughed uncomfortably. "Well, next time maybe me and you and her can enjoy ourselves together-er, ah never mind."

The front door opened slowly and the doughy wiggly Dan stepped out. He carefully closed the door behind him as to prevent a psychosomatic sergeant from appearing and insulting his impoliteness.

He was wearing his standard uniform, anime t-shirt and cargo shorts with sandals. He wore this all year long, even in snow storms, but today his outfit actually coincided with the weather.

It took a moment for his hangover demons to leave before he had the clarity to acknowledge us. His face went from a squint to an even harder sun-in-my-eyes squint. "What are you guys doing?" he asked.

"What does it look like?" asked Phishy.

126

"Standing."

Phishy snapped back. "Yep, want to join us?"

"Okay."

He came down and stood with us, not saying a word. He seemed very comfortable to the fact that we were all looking at him, also not saying a word. He was once again occupied with whatever his internal monologue was judging him on today. However, to us it appeared to be a man propagating an ear splitting silence because of the dimness of his mind.

"How's it going, Dan?" asked God.

"Oh, very well, ma'am."

"That's good."

The front door opened again and Laura Foster whimpered with a hangover as she stepped out the door. Her wet hair and outfit consisting of Phishy's clothes meant she left a "present" in his bed.

When she finally realized all but one of us were watching her she stopped and looked back. A smile of pleasure and confusion spread across her face. "What? What are you guys looking at? What is it? TELL ME!"

"Nothing," said Nik.

She rubbed her eyes and half cried. "What are you guys doing out here?"

"Cleaning; you should help," said Phishy.

She looked around for an excuse, but the seven people on the lawn waiting to judge her inhibited her from sneaking out of this chore. Peer pressure won again and she stepped down to assist us whenever we actually got started.

"Hey, Phishy," said Laura. "I'm sorry but I had to borrow some clothes. I hope you don't mind. You have a lot of cool posters in there by the way."

"Yeah? Well I mean, as long as you didn't vomit all over my bed." He rolled his eyes; he already knew.

She made the nicest face she could make and said, "Well…"

Phishy dropped his garbage bag and stomped around the yard with his hands flying in the air. "God Dammit! Every goddamn time you guys got to make a goddamn mess in my goddamn room! Why the hell do I let you guys come over?"

She squished her body as tightly as she could, for she wanted to disappear into another dimension. She began to pity cry as she spoke. "I'm sorry! I pulled up the sheets and pillows I messed up! And I wiped up a bunch of it off the carpet and walls."

He put his hands on the sides of his face and yelled. "ON THE WALLS? HOW THE FUCK DID YOU GET PUKE ON MY WALLS?"

"I don't know, okay? I'm sorry."

Phishy walked away and faced the street. He was so angry he couldn't even look at her. "Well you're cleaning that up, dammit."

She shuttered at the thought. "Ew, do I have to?"

He turned around and faced her. "YES!" he yelled.

"Can't we hire somebody? I'm pretty sure there's companies that clean up after parties."

"No! I hate it when you guys do this!"

I put my hand on Phishy's shoulder. "Hey, man. Relax," I said calmly. "It's basically tradition. Besides, it only ever gets clean when we force you to do it."

He shook his head. "No way; I clean my room all the time!"

The door opened again and Alexander Peliolagos, eldest of the four Pelio children, stepped out. He had no outstanding clothing or grooming. It could be said that Alex had the face of someone that could easily be lost in a crowd, even by people that knew him. Looking at us, he lifted his indescribable hand into an indescribable shape, as if to say something.

"Shut up, Alex. Get down here," said God, second of the Pelio children and vice-mother of Alex

He walked down in an indescribable way and stood there. He may have said something but it was not important.

The front door of the Ortega residence busted open and a half-drunk ogre stomped out with a nearly empty bottle of tequila in his hand. His red Mohawk was down and his shirt was missing, which revealed his chiseled, ripped, freckled body. The armaments of the dreadnaught that was Michael Rose were fully exposed, ready to push a weight up and down, or whatever they were used for. His stretch-mark laden milky white skin seemed wet as he pounded the ground towards us.

"Why are you all wet?" asked Will.

"It fucking rained in there. I almost drowned," he grunted.

"Bullshit. You probably woke yourself up by accidently kicking the shower faucet on," I said.

He was gripping his hangover head. "No, it was a hurricane."

"Why did you pass out in the shower, Gunshow?" asked God.

"Probably to get some water so I don't have a killer hangover. Hey, did any of you guys wake up with your pants down? I did and I wanted to know if I got any last night or it was some game. I hope it was that Laura chick; she's hot as fuck."

"Ha ha, wow, ha, really?" said Laura as she looked around, half-embarrassed.

Gunshow was surprised to see her. "Shit, if I knew you were here I would have been more uh, subble-stubble-suptle—"

"Subtle?" said God.

"Yeah, Sautul."

"Actually, yeah, I did have my pants down," said Jerry. "I was passed out in the backyard alone. I thought I might a have fooled around with that Jackie girl."

"Me too. I was in Phishy's room," said Dan.

"I was in the kitchen," said Nik.

"I was in Phishy's brother's room," said Will.

Alex said something at this point, but it didn't matter.

"I was also in the kitchen," said Phishy.

"B-but nothing happened," replied Nik.

"I wanted to use Phishy's brother's room but it was locked, so I slept outside the door. Also, I kept my pants on," said God.

"I was in the basement, pants off," I said.

129

We looked at Megan, who did not want to reveal her post-partydom location. After a few seconds of staring, she opened up. "I was uh, uh, in the back seat of Brian's car. The door was wide open when I woke up."

"Did you have your pants down?" asked Gunshow.

"I was wearing a black dress."

"Yeah, but was it down?"

"Uh, you mean up? Uh, no I was uh…still wearing it."

"Ooh, what were you doing in Ammo's car?' asked Phishy like a fourteen year-old girl.

"Hold on, guys," I said. "Nothing happened. I do not recall any events taking place in my car."

Then I winked at her. I winked because I was telling her that 'don't worry, I know you're uncomfortable and I've got your back' and she could relax. The wink *also* said 'ya' know, I'm not against the idea'. I wasn't trying to be like Jerry, but I wasn't going to close a door on a cute girl either. I winked for the present situation, and for the future. My mind was on a railroad for Portland, Maine where her thoughts can meet mine there. This wink however just said 'Portland' and she went to Portland, Oregon, the wrong way and further from the truth.

She took this wink as the truth that I was only going to show her, and my friends were left with a lie that was only meant to put her in a positive light. This wink told her that we actually did have a sexual interaction in the back of my car, just like how every other first time occurred.

She also had evidence that she did in fact have intercourse with someone, but this was something I did not know at the time. This is also something I didn't know *later* but something I inferred much later in life.

Her face was strange; I couldn't read it. Hindsight told me that it was an uneasy acceptance mixed with a validation to her fears, but I could not identify this very important moment. I saw her body sink to the tune of the misunderstanding; her legs stepped together, her head tilted downward, and her muscles relaxed for what was probably going to last a month. Then her heart would race for hours until it would drop to the slow tune of depression, a sonnet it would never escape from.

130

I should have known something was up. If I did then everything might have been different, but then again, she went this way, and never truly asked for directions. She was scared, she was disappointed, and I could have done more, but she didn't cry loud enough for help. I wanted to chalk this up to a misunderstanding because then she seemed smarter, stronger, and healthier. I wanted her to lack the agency of her own life so her actions could seem more pure— more like how I felt about her. I wanted her to be the damsel I just couldn't save. I wanted to blame this wink and then blame myself because then I wouldn't have to blame her.

Rainstorms, August 1st

Why was her hand on the faucet? Why did my mind insist on such a tiny detail? Was it because it was the last thing Laura said about her? Did my mind decide to skip over and over with its little unstoppable scratch simply because that was the end of the record? Or was it deeper—a puzzle within the unconscious of my own mind that was struggling to parlay the assistance of its shell shocked conscience brother? Was the reach some sort of symbol to outline what she was feeling and thinking before the dancing darkness courted her soul? Or was that detail my monkey brain's only refuge from the grinding nihilism that followed an unexpected calamity?

I knew this fact didn't matter, yet I held onto it. It was the only thing she couldn't take away from me. She didn't know how much she betrayed me and the world for her cut losses. She thought this was the way to set me free from her dissention into a lightless void, yet I was forced onto this foreign shore with nothing but holes in my heart. I wanted nothing more than to dive back in and swim through the trillions of gallons to pull her out.

Unfortunately, she gave me no chance, no opinion. If this was a violent act of nature, there would be no ill will and I could see her act as the veil from harm she was convinced to be. This was not a sacrifice, for even the humblest of martyrs at least provide some notification before they discharge their services.

What I held in my hands was her reason—her excuse—to justify and answer for the sins she committed. She said she was a demon that choose every wrong turn and fell so far away that she lost the grace she was given.

She tainted a child—a child that was already going to be burdened with an unknown father. She must have thought her alcohol poisoning beneath the rain would remove the situation, the deep scar that only she could see. She would have needed to live a life of perpetual distractions, but a life, at least for a while, worth living. Instead the child's tenacity cost two lives instead of one.

That was what her note said. It also said things like: I will always love you, you will achieve so much in your life, I will watch over you and everyone else I love, this had to be done, and don't blame yourself. So the rest was nothing but the cherry flavor around the medicine. Except for don't blame yourself, that's the catalyst that ignited my rage. I *wanted* to blame myself, and every other thought was finding a way to make me the bad guy, but I couldn't, and it just made her appear worse.

When Laura handed me her note, I couldn't even open it. After the obvious "What's wrong?" and "I'm sorry, Brian" stuff, I put the note into my pocket to read alone. I thought it was better for me to hear the facts first then read why after so I could have some context. Instead, it left me sour and even more heartbroken. I saw that maybe if I read her note first, I wouldn't find any peace, but at least I might have given Megan and her unborn child some pity.

Laura of course didn't read the note; otherwise she probably would have thrown it away out of horror. I could see the confusion mixed deeply into the sadness, so Megan still held some nobility within Laura.

Laura told me that she was found in the bathtub. The shower was on and by the time her father found her, the water was running out of the bathroom and down the stairs. The tub itself was extra-large. Large enough for her to be completely suspended beneath the water and still have enough room to drift around.

Her body wanted to resurface, but the casts on her legs held her down. I was told that the result of this was that she appeared to be floating within the water, and her white dress fanned out across the tub, enveloping her in a shroud. Aside from the marked comments on her casts that slowly dissolved within the water, she was completely surrounded in white.

I asked about her eyes. They were open, but her face was nearly expressionless. It was shaped as if she were about to innocently pose a question. What she would have asked, and who would have received the question is beyond the discovery of mortals.

What perplexed me was her right hand, which was the only piece of her that was out of the water. It was lifted above her head upon the hot water knob. The thing was that the knob was not turned all the way. If she turned it to the right, the rain that was falling upon her would have arrived harder and hotter. If she turned the knob to the left, the scalding storm would have ended and all she needed to do was lift the drain plug to save her life.

She did ingest a lot of pain pills; an empty bottle was found by toilet. However, Laura would tell me later that the coroner stated that although Megan did overdose, it was not enough to kill her. She would have passed out, and if she hadn't gotten into the tub, she might still be alive. Alive so I could ask what the hell happened.

Ascension, August 6th

The dark cold glow of the storm clouds illuminated Megan into a pale, zombie-like tone. Whatever makeup that was on her to give her some vital colors only amplified her state of death. The red on her cheeks and around her eyes only portrayed her as some sort of cheap doll, complete with chipping skin and disappearing hair.

To further hide the waterlogged corpse, a white veil was placed over her head. A white lacy dress that went from her chin, down her arms, and most likely her legs was definitely an expensive and well-crafted outfit for any living person. Unfortunately, she looked more like a post-modern art piece about marriage and feminism then a sleeping beauty.

Her coffin was a fancy red wood I couldn't identify, but I knew it was pricey. Inside the coffin were white silk cushions upholstered with little black gemstones. Surrounding her were white lilies and white daisies carefully arranged as to imply that she was in a meadow. There was a reef of more white flowers on the coffin and a white ribbon was wrapped around the handles.

The building containing the wake was a pretty typical funeral home. The walls were an old stained wood that had large, but high up windows. The 70's teal curtains did match the rug with a well cleaned, yet dated carpet. The room had about fifty seats and two dozen or so were occupied by various people I did and didn't know. Around the room were more and more arrangements of white flowers with pictures of Megan throughout different stages of her life.

There were pictures of her swimming in her pool from around the age of 2 until the age of 18. There were a lot of pictures of her playing with her dog Sunday, which was a St. Bernard. There were pictures of her doing random things either alone or with her sister like baking, playing, singing, and laying in the sun. There were also quite a few pictures that were

135

irregularly cut. These photos occasionally had an arm or leg sticking out, which I assumed to be her mother's.

God walked up to me. She was in a black dress with dark stockings and black high heels. Her black curly hair was actually styled with side bangs that rested on her black framed glasses. Of course she was concerned, and had a drink to offer me.

"Hey, Ammo." Her condolences seeped through every letter

"Hey." Failed disinterest seeped through mine

"I'm sorry."

"It's not your fault, God."

"I know, I just… I want you to know that I feel for you and if you need anything I'm here. And the rest of us are outside on the porch. And also you should stop playing with your tie. It's starting to look weird."

I put down the tie. The wrinkles twisted it into a lumpy spiral. "Why aren't you guys in here?"

"You know why."

I gave a frustrated sigh. "Jeeze, you guys can't wait until we're at Phishy's? Or at least in the car?"

"I agree, and I'm not drinking. It's mostly Gunshow, Dan, and Phishy. The rest of us are just hanging out."

I looked away in disbelief. I didn't want them screwing around and disrespecting the woman I was so pissed off at. I left God even though I knew it wasn't her fault.

I sat next to Laura, who was crying profusely alone in the corner. She was wearing a little black dress that looked more appropriate in a club. The eight or nine handkerchiefs on the seat next to her were soaked. I sat on the chair on the other side.

"H-hello, A-ammo," she said in between tears.

"Hello, Laura. Your family did a very nice job with her; she looks very peaceful."

"Yeah, the white was my idea. She never wanted anyone to be sad on her part. I thought the white would look less depressing."

Maybe if she didn't kill herself nobody would be upset. Instead she exploded her misery on everyone that cared about her.

"It is nice. So why are you all alone? Where's your father?"

"I don't know. He was pretty upset but okay. Then he got this phone call and told me he needed to leave. I've never seen him so upset."

"Well he's the sheriff of Aberdeen County, so it must have been work stuff. I would be livid as well if I had to work during my daughter's wake."

"I know. I want him here though."

Although the talking calmed her down, the crying picked right up again the moment I stopped. I tried to think of anything to say.

"So where's Gunshow?" I asked. "Isn't he here?"

"Yes, and I really want him with me, but my dad would kill him if he saw Gunshow even near me. We both agree that it's best if he stays back. Besides, he's taking me out to dinner after the funeral."

"That's nice. Where are you guys going? Laura? Laura?"

She completely ignored me. Her whole body froze solid, shocked at whoever was looking over the corpse. After some time, the lady turned around and walked towards us.

The woman was most likely in her late forties, but years of exposure to the sun gave her some extra wrinkles around her face. She had a reddish tan with sunspots on her chest, or at least the part that was reviled by her black tank and blazer combo. Her hair was light brown, curly, short, and dry from years on a beach. She had black jeans and black boots, both worn from years of irresponsibility.

"Hello, Laura," she said with the low voice of a calm smoker chick.

Laura didn't respond; she was still paralyzed.

She brushed her hair over her ear and took a deep breath before speaking to Laura. "I'm so sorry. I'm so sorry I left. I tried to contact you girls but your father kept intercepting me. He even tried to stop me from coming here."

"I-uh-I," Laura replied without any movement of her face.

"I've always loved you girls. I wish so damn hard just to see Megan alive one more time. I just want to go back in time and tell her I love her one more time, but I can't." She got down on one knee to be at eye level with a petrified Laura. Every regret she had flooded into the expression on her face. Every wrinkle did its part to fold her flesh into a window of incomparable emotional trauma.

"So I can only make it up to you. Please Laura, let me be in your life. You're a grown woman now and your father can't keep us apart any longer. Please, please, please let me talk to you."

Laura's face moved slowly and inconsistently like her mind had to relearn how to move the muscles. After some stuttering she finally spoke. "Why now?" she snapped. "Megan's been in college for years yet you never contacted her! She was a grown woman too!"

"I know, I know. You girls were raised so religiously that I actually believed your father when he told me you thought I was a demon. I'm not asking for any forgiveness–I deserve none. And if you want to blame me for Megan's death, then I accept that too. Just give me the option to be in your life."

Laura began to breathe heavily as the rage built up in her. "What? I don't even want to call you mother! I don't even want to see you! Fuck you! Fuck you! *Fuck you*!"

I leaned away from them to show all of the people that were now looking at us that I was just an innocent bystander.

The lady tried to put her hands on Laura's hands, but Laura ripped them away. Both of them were breaking out in violent tears, but the lady's cries were louder.

"Please, Laura! I have to go back tonight but I want to see you again! I will fly you out to my home in Marseille! I will pay for everything! I will take care of you! I will show you Europe! I will do everything I can for you! Please! Please, let

138

me be the mother I should have been!" She laid her head practically on Laura's lap.

Laura pushed her back and stood up above her. "I wanted to see you for so long and now I want to break your fucking skull! I'm not going out there! You are the biggest bitch I have ever fucking known! The only thing I want from you is to suffer—for me, but especially for Megan."

The lady stumbled to her feet and put her arms on Laura's shoulders. "Please, I have done a horrible thing to you, but let me fix it! I am your mother! Please let me at least see my daughter one last time! I will give anything to be with you! I will give anything to earn your love again!"

Laura knocked off the lady's arms and turned away from her. "The mother I had left me ten years ago. The mother I had isn't worth loving anymore. Please leave; you're too much for me right now."

The lady stood up straight and wiped off her tears. She reached into her blazer and pulled out a business card. "This is my number; please call me. I'm so sorry I upset you. I love you Laura."

She dropped the card on Laura's chair and walked out of the room. After a moment of silence, I believed Laura needed to be alone so I went out a different way than the lady to meet up with my friends.

The rain picked up a little outside, but the large awning kept me and the others on the deck from getting wet. The air was nice and cool, which was more than refreshing.

On the deck, Dan and God were crying together into a bottle of tequila. Gunshow was stoically looking out into the rain as he silently sipped vodka. Phishy was talking to Jerry as Jerry tried to sit alone with his thoughts. Will stood there, watching them all.

"God, I thought you weren't going to drink!" I said sternly.

"I'm sorry, Ammo, but I couldn't take it. I'm just so sad and I miss her so much. Please, have some too," said God between the tears.

I threw my hands out and said, "No."

Dan suddenly got up and ran off the deck and into the rain. In the distance I heard him hurling loudly.

"I am so disappointed," I said, staring out into the rain.

"Well this is how we cope," said God apologetically. "Everyone should be able to deal with loss in their own way. I am sorry we offend you, Ammo."

Phishy got up and took a swig from his own tequila bottle. "Yeah, you need to relax. Here I'll pour one for the homies." He poured the last quarter of his drink onto the floor. I starred at the puddle for about ten seconds before I was ready to look Phishy in the eyes.

"So I'm sorry to budge in here, but I have something to say," said Will. "I'm going to Japan."

We all stopped and looked at him. Except for Gunshow—he was still posing with his thoughts.

"Can't you see I'm in mourning? We can wait for your weeaboo crap later," said Phishy.

God got up and fumbled over to Will. She put her bottle arm around him. With her other hand she adjusted her heel that she was clearly not used to wearing. "I'm so glad for you. When are you leaving?" she asked with an optimistic slur.

"Three weeks," he replied.

"Wow, that is quick. When are you coming home?"

"The plan is pretty much never. I'm going to be an architect out there."

Phishy butted in and grabbed the limelight. "Well, Jerry and I are going on our road trip. We'll be leaving in three weeks as well."

Jerry snapped back to Earth "Yep, uh, hitting it out."

Adam Foster, Laura's father, walked up the steps and passed us. He gave a very disapproving look at Phishy. Phishy pulled a little bottle of tequila from his back pocket and took a few gulps. He held the rest up to Adam's mouth "Hey, mister Megan's dad, you sure could use a drink. Here, open your mouth so you don't get any of my germs."

His eyes went from an intimidating stare to a scowl that could shatter bones. I could see all of the blood leave his heart and enter his hairless head and hairy fists. The rest of us

140

vanished into the darkness that consumed the world. All that remained was a red spotlight that illuminated a drunk and disorderly Phishy and a beast that was chained up inside a sheriff's body. The air throughout the universe held still as the rage consumed the man.

"Who are you?" said Mr. Foster with eyes so intense they looked like they were going to burst out.

"Oh, well I'm Raul Ortega. I was Megan's friend," replied Phishy ignorantly.

"Raul, she was often at your house, correct? For example, her 21st birthday?"

Phishy was confused; whatever he expected from Adam, that wasn't it. "Oh, uh yeah."

"Is it the one in that unfinished subdivision in Kirkman?"

"Yeah."

"So tell me, as her friend, what do you remember about her? Or does the alcohol make you too stupid to remember?"

"Not at all. I remember giving her first shot at her 21st. I remember letting her have some molly at her pool party. I remember—ha ha, grinding dat ass on the dance floor. I remember her getting laid in my driveway. I remember her calling me and asking how many pain pills she should take to feel real good. So yeah, the alcohol doesn't affect me at all, Mister Megan's dad."

All of us on that deck had eyes so wide they should have fallen out. Any one of us could have stopped him, but the more words that rolled out of his accursed mouth made it a better and better idea to create as much distance from him as possible. Besides, Mr. Foster didn't know our group dynamic so for all he knew Phishy was some lone wolf that was drinking with some other shitfaced kids at a wake.

Mr. Foster actually didn't look that upset. I suppose he had so much rage in his head that it must have split his brain open and poured out. What was left was a man with no facial expression, but on the inside experienced every emotion during the 30 seconds he stared at Phishy. "I'm going to decline that drink for now," he said. "I think I will save it for later."

Tuna Can, August 14th

I didn't think I'd ever seen God cry that hard. She had to deal with two funerals for two close friends with only a week apart. Her head was buried in my shoulder as she wept as silently as she could. Her hand was squeezing mine, and if there wasn't such a strength difference between us, she would have smashed it.

She tried to be polite, and it's not like she was stealing the show, which would anger an even dead Phishy, but a few people acknowledged her crying. It might have been easier if the event wasn't in Spanish. Then she could at least have been distracted by the meaningful words of the family and the hollow words of the priest. Instead, her mind had to swim with the fact that her oldest childhood friend suddenly died from a shotgun blast to the chest.

She was clever though; it was only going to take a few days for her mind to reason out this situation. Then I would see her again as the opinionated, anorexic dreamer I'd known for almost half my life.

There were other people crying as well so God was not alone. Mostly women and children, for it was far too unmanly for El Salvadorian men to cry. Of my other friends, only Gunshow, Jerry, Dan, and Will came with and none of them were going to cry—at least not without a few drinks.

The funeral itself was a very standard affair. Everything was as it was from every movie with a funeral scene. It had the grassy cemetery, cloudy skies, and everyone in black. Like all of Mrs. Ortega's designs, this one lacked individuality.

I was surprised to see Phishy's brother. Not that he wasn't about the family, but all he ever showed toward Phishy was animosity. He of course had the nicest suit, that of course was custom made by some guy in of course, Los Angeles. The perfect cuts made him look better than his blond aspiring actress

143

girlfriend. Just by how he sat I could see him somehow finding a way to turn this into yet another exercise in ego inflation.

During the funeral my phone not-so-quietly vibrated with a message from Raj. I quickly responded with a "nope" even though I didn't read it. Knowing that he would call me, I silenced my phone. I was sick of the constant interruptions, especially when I had so little time left in the valley. I'll probably quit too, but I'm not going to waste my brainpower thinking about it now.

After the funeral ended and everyone returned to their cars, my friends and I gathered in a circle to collect our thoughts. Dan and Gunshow already lifted out their utility hooch and passed it around. Everyone took a few swigs. I did as well, for I grew exhausted to the events surrounding me. When the booze got to God, she downed half the bottle before passing it along.

"So what are they going to do with Adam Foster?" asked Jerry.

Every gulp Dan took made him weep a little more and more.

"He turned himself in, so he's probably going to jail for life," said Gunshow.

"Good, fucking hypocrite. For a man who listens to Jesus all the time he sure knows how to fucking sin," declared God.

"What's going to happen to Laura?" asked Will. "She's all alone now, right?"

"She's been staying at my place," said Gunshow "Mom's real cool about it. And Robbie's been back for a few weeks so he's been helping us too."

"Robbie Red Rose? Your brother who used to torture squirrels?" asked Jerry.

"No, that was my other brother Todd. Robbie was the one who lit his girlfriend's hair on fire, and his pants, and all of my stuffed animals, and the toilet paper in school."

"Damn, and he's helping you?" asked Will.

"Well, the military really busted his balls so now he flies right."

"Yeah, his brothers sucked. Remember when Todd built a potato gun and shot Robbie in the nuts?" I asked.

"Fuck yeah, Robbie couldn't walk for weeks. My dad beat Todd so hard he broke his fingers," replied Gunshow.

"It's funny now, but those dudes were fucking awful when we were kids," said God.

"Yeah, like after Robbie tried to steal your socks and huff them," I said.

"Uh, yeah. Good thing he was smaller than me. He was the first man I gave two black eyes and missing teeth," she replied.

"The first?" asked Jerry.

God wiped some tears from her eyes. The friends and alcohol was putting her at ease. "Well I'm only 21. I have many years to stop sexual abuse by aggressive men," she said.

"Hey, guys, not to be rude but we should discuss our memories of Phishy, not the Black and Red Roses," I said.

We were quiet for a while until God laughed a bit and brought up a memory. "Remember that time Phishy was obsessed with that gay porn parody?"

"Yeah," I said, "and he kept showing people it in school. He would laugh his ass off while everyone else cringed."

"It was fucking gross. I told him if he showed me that shit one more time I'd snap his fucking phone in half," added Gunshow.

"And he did," I said.

"And I fucking snapped it."

When the bottle came back to me I took a swig and passed. Deep down I was still miserable, but misery loves company. And I was around the best people to share it with.

The Slag, August 20th

The only time the internet is amazing is when I have better things to do. Whenever I'm sitting around and have nothing but internet time, it's all junk. No good threads, videos, articles, or images. It sucks to because I was locked to my window, waiting for Gunshow, God, and Laura. And because of the recent events, I didn't think I should have appeared reclusive. So there I was, half looking out the window and half looking at a slow day on the web.

It was cloudy with a little bit of drizzle, just enough to make the day a bit too cold for August. Good thing I was going to get in Gunshow's little pickup. Pete used to call it the "Bulletwagon" because it was the same model used by guerilla warriors in Africa and Asia. It didn't help that Gunshow's wagon contained a few holes from the older Roses.

Then I heard it, off in the distance. Fuck. My eyes widened. I knew I wasn't getting in the Bulletwagon. The sound grew louder and louder. Dammit, I didn't want to worry about dying today. My heart began to race as the roars of a zombie machine echoed throughout my neighborhood. As it turned on my street, the hiss twisted around my ears. It was a hiss that cursed every child that witnessed it. Crap, I wished they warned me. I needed to prepare for the nightmare, the horror, the danger, The Slag.

The four horsemen of the apocalypse will not arrive on horses. Instead they will carpool in The Slag. It was a culmination of the Peliolagos curse bound together in a abomination more relatable to a terrestrial flotsam than an automobile.

The paint mostly survived as a black base with two white stripes along the top. Almost matching black spray-paint covered the rusted body in pockets along the edges and bondo'd holes along the skirt. The front bumper was held up with tie-die duct tape left to fade in the sun while the back was suspended

146

with bungee cords from the trunk. The license plates rested in their respective windows due to all of the screws that would have held them up being stripped. Only two hubcaps remained, and of course they didn't match.

All of the lights legally worked, but all of the back right lights were shattered while the front left dangled out of its socket, waiting for some robot vulture to snatch it up. It had a sunroof of shattered glass so the glare guard was the only thing preventing the rain, which it did a horrible job doing. The right side mirror was false. It was a sort of fun-house mirror material that was applied to avoid police. Meanwhile, the other side was just gone. The gas cap and cover were removed, so there was an open hole into the gas chamber. Finally, the signature sound came from the detached muffler. A wrench was wedged between the broken pipes to keep them from falling onto the street.

I climbed in through the "window" and sat down in the back "seat".

"Hey, Ammo," said God in a positive kindergarten teacher voice.

"Hey. I thought Gunshow was picking me up?" I said in a suspicious professor voice.

She faced the road as she unenthusiastically spoke to me. "Nah, he wanted to get a head start on moving."

The outside was an embarrassment, but the interior was a terror. The formally fuzzy formally blue upholstery was covered in a rainbow of stains and smudges. Cigarette butts covered every crevice and a pile was left in the right cup holder. The left cup holder held a murky swamp left untouched by man for over ten years, its treasure of unfortunate quarters waiting to be plundered. The top of the steering wheel lost its cushion and left the metal exposed, ready to burn or freeze depending on the season. The turn signals either worked or buzzed like the wrong answer on a game show. Only part of the dashboard lit up, so nighttime driving beyond 35 mph was left to a guessing game. The gas gauge was broken in the dead center, so an often forgotten gas can was in the trunk. The cassette player was gone, as in not there. The A/C gave a loud, agonizing hiss until it actually began to chill after fifteen minutes.

After a long silence God spoke up again. "What do you think will happen to him?"

Damn, it's only been a few days but it feels like I haven't thought about that in forever. Grieving never lasts as long as you want it to, but otherwise it could last forever.

"Well he turned himself in. Also, he's a cop, so at least a few years," I looked out the window, hoping that a meteor would fly down and destroy us so I wouldn't have to talk about this.

She sighed. "That's so unfortunate. Maybe the judge will give him life?"

"I don't think so. He was also drunk, so he could pull the crime of passion card."

"That's true."

The passenger window didn't work because it was held up by a board—there was no panel on the door. All of the inner wiring and mechanics were exposed as the rust slowly creeped around the door from the outside. To exit, a monkey wrench was needed to turn a bolt to lift the heavy metal bar holding it in place. That was the least of the passenger's problems due to an ink bucket holding up the already uncomfortable seat, and the lack of a proper seat belt. The current one was a rope used to tie the passenger to the chair. The foot rests were plastic mats attached to the floor, however, the passenger one had been smashed through, exposing it to the road below. At one point the vehicle was driven through some farm fields, because corn husks and alfalfa were still jammed in the corners.

Like an uncomfortable taxi passenger I spoke up again. "Even still, his life is ruined. He's never going to get a good job as a murderer."

Her voice went from a guarded monotone to an opera monologue. "I know, right? I mean, it makes me happy in this case but so many lives are ruined by our draconian laws. This country imprisons more people than China, Russia, or Iran! We have this huge hate for people that make mistakes so we just tell them they're worthless and deny them any chance of

148

contributing to society! How can we call ourselves a nation when we care for no one outside of our family? Smoked a joint when you were 11? Well fuck you 'till the day you die! Clearly you lack the morals to do anything productive with your life! Unless you run a church!"

I actually laughed a little. "Okay now, are you moving to Sweden tonight or tomorrow?"

"Ha, it's Norway I'm moving to."

Unless the car was moving, the situation in the vehicle changed to a dramatic vibration comparable to the reentry of a rocket. The shaking would even loosen the breaks to the point of a slow lurch forward. It would also rattle two of the three surviving metal door handles (the third was smashed open so it needed to be locked at all times to prevent perpetual ajarness).

I leaned forward to speak to her. "You said it makes you happy that Adam Foster is suffering but it almost sounds like you still pity him."

She took a moment for an answer. "I don't. He's now in a group I do pity though. So I guess he gets some collateral pity? Either way I hope he rots."

It was a while before I spoke again. "I wonder how Laura feels about him."

"Betrayed and alone. She won't see him at all. And I don't think she's going to stay in contact with him."

"So now everyone in her family betrayed her."

"No, her extended family is helping her sell the house and give her all of the money. She's so strong."

"Stronger than Megan," I replied under my breath

"Yeah. We're also her support group. If she needs anything me or Gunshow will help her out."

"That's nice of you guys. And at least she's distracted by the move."

"Yeah, distractions makes everything better."

"Distractions only help when you should be doing something else.

The Victorian Era, August 20th

Victoria was once a town that had it all, and it was getting less and less by the day. Veterans of the Second World War used their GI bill money on the new neighborhoods of the exploding Victoria suburb. Every hour a new piece of the American dream opened up for a nice pleasant family. A man walked in to start a nest of wholesome experiences like women working, children experimenting with drugs, raving parities, abuse, and painting. They left their foundations in the cities and countryside for the rank and file boxes and commercials that would eat the utility and culture of the generations to come. Or not, despite the trend of cold war America to homogenize its citizen's, the inherent individualism of the human animal combined with the infinitely diverse problems of said citizens prevented a true assimilation found only in television. Either way, the identical boxes of angles and windows was a moment of pride captured in the decaying municipality of Victoria.

The arrogance of Victoria's generation required an understanding found outside of the streets, but was expressed by the weathered signs that stood within them. The televisions, politians, marches, and Christmas jingles promoted a moral superiority found in their culture that the future generations failed to achieve, and will ultimately doom America. The baby boomers were too selfish, the gen X'ers were too weak, the Millennials were too thoughtless, and the Z'ers were too shy. They were the Greatest generation, and this title would be the best way to express the generation of who they really were if anyone realized they gave themselves that title. Unfortunately, nostalgia removed any impurities that generation had, and left behind false idols that would forever insult and belittle the inheriting generations.

Never mind it was the Greatest generation that started America's chemical dependence, was complacent in the current mantra of selfishness of corporations, encouraged the destruction of the environment for present-day profit, and seeded every immoral movement they themselves resented. Like the managers of any organization, the people beneath them were the ones to blame for their own problems.

This is what I saw when I entered the town: an extremely loud hypocrisy everyone is too deaf to hear. That the swing line signs and dancing light bulb lights that promoted Latin businesses and culture was somehow a failure. The ghost town that would have been the future of this place without the waves of immigration was somehow a disappointment everyone else should feel sorry for.

These little tonal shifts in the song of Victoria could be found everywhere. Little white boxy grocery stores with thick rusty shopping carts still had the title of "Ralph's", or "Bob's', or "Jimmy's" groceries even though the insides consisted of products primarily written in Spanish. The parking lots shifted from state-of-the-art metal boxes with fins and leather seats to decade-old plastic cartons with spinning rims. The swanky strip malls and roadhouses drifted from burgers and fries to tacos and rice. The South Korea aged sidewalks and roads slowly chipped away, splintering and braking into disappointing and dangerous cobblestone pathways. Back in the day, American flags waved from the porch of every other house and one by one, each came down and a Mexican or Cuban or El Salvadorian one took its place.

There were some living remnants of the imaginary past. With their veteran hats and slow moving vehicles, they complained about how America was over and everyone else messed it up. Their children listened, and saw how the thick brick and concrete buildings of their hometown were filled with people they didn't know. Then they scattered the hormone-deficient rants of their parents into the winds of the media so everyone could believe how much everyone else had failed.

"Hey, Ammo. You've been pretty quiet," said God.

"Yeah, well don't I deserve to be? My sort-of girlfriend and one of my best friends are dead," I replied.

"I know. They were my friends too. I just wanted to make sure you're okay."

"I'm not going to kill myself."

"Fuck, Ammo. I didn't think you would. But we all need each other—you included. We all need to care for each other because this is difficult."

"I was there when Phishy got shot. I was. And I ran. I didn't even check on him. I just ran. I didn't even think about where I was going. I just ran."

She thought about that for a moment. God always had an opinion so this pause was serious.

"I'm glad you left. What could you have achieved but have been killed as well? There was nothing you could have done for him. I mean, he got a shotgun blast to the chest."

"Yeah, whatever."

"You just want to blame yourself so life and death don't seem so meaningless and we actually have any control over what happens to us. Because no control is simply too terrifying."

"Thanks, God. Now I'm sad *and* helpless."

"Hey, that's what I learned in my philosophy class. And honestly, it's kind of liberating knowing we have no control."

"We have control; I could pick up smoking and die of lung cancer."

"But you would only do that to prove me wrong, thus proving me right. And if you did this in the real world without this conversation, then you would have only picked up smoking because someone else told you it was cool. See? You have no control. Nobody does."

I rolled over in my seat, but not too much, for whatever held up this seat could not be very stable. "Well I want control." I said.

"And I want some weed."

"Yeah, that's just as good."

"It's not, but it feels like it is."

I examined the door beside me. The little abscesses of rust crumbled apart as I rubbed my finger across them. "What are we but our feelings?" I asked

"Logical? Productive? Fair?" she responded.

"Empty?"

"You have feelings now, and you're still empty."

"You're right. I should become a robot. I could be a forklift, and move boxes from the left to the right. That's progress."

"And then I'll be a magic 8 ball, but my only response would be maybe."

"Ha, then Gunshow could be a fighter jet that only drops F bombs."

"Laura could be a music box that never stops playing."

"Nik could be an air horn that only works when you're relaxing."

"God, despite your bizarre philosophy of man, you still make me feel good."

"Ammo, you always have something to say tucked away."

We stopped at the corner of Mall and JFK Avenue. It was called this because at the time Victoria built the largest mall in the nation. None other John F. Kennedy dropped by to give a speech on it just before he left for Houston. Victoria was so proud to finally have some history that they changed the name of Main Street the day after the speech. It must have been weird for a while after he died.

The mall itself was big and wooden, and like all big wooden things that are referred to in the past tense, it burned down. Ironically the fire occurred in December, during a snow storm. A shop with one too many Christmas lights plugged into one too few outlets caused some sparks to fall onto a too shaggy of a carpet.

The fire swarmed the inside area and both fortunately and unfortunately no one was around so the fire already seized control of half of the mall before anyone noticed. The firefighters were called out but the fire spread to the outside before they even got there. Everything from the arcades, to the roller rinks, to the bookstores burned to the ground. The firefighters new this and spent their energy keeping the fire from spreading to the other buildings.

What was left of the jewel of Victoria was a field of ashes and horrifyingly melted animatronic Santas. An ice rink and bowling alley did survive the blaze but a bad recession hit the following year and everyone moved onto different pastimes like cocaine.

What stood today were some soccer fields on the outskirts of downtown. The fields were surrounded by prairie plants, which must have started out as just weeds and morphed into a rather pleasant piece of environmentalism.

"I think you're going to like the place. From the living room you can see the river, and from my room you can see downtown," said God.

"Whoa, it's like you're living the high life. Can Gunshow see lake Michigan from his toilet?"

"Why are you being an ass? You were fine like two minutes ago."

"I remembered life sucks."

"I remembered *you* suck."

"Why am I even coming? Gunshow still won't talk to me directly, which will make things difficult when we carry the couches up the stairs."

"Well I'll talk to him. Then he'll punch you. Then you'll cry. Then it will be all better. Understand?"

"Yes, my Goddess."

"Asshat."

Downtown was formally a housewife's dream. Shops upon shops upon shops adorned with beautiful modernist buildings. Blocks of two and three-story structures surrounded the visitor and provided the feeling of a little Chicago inside of a family friendly suburb. Every railing, parking meter, and bench had an art deco style with harsh curves and poppy shapes. The designers successfully built an area with a feeling separate from the rest of the Aberdeen valley.

At the center of it all stood Weismann tower, a building which at twenty stories dwarfed the other four and five story buildings in the rest of the city. It was tall and slender, taking up as much space on the ground as a large restaurant. It wasn't square either; it had a shape that was too irregular for a name, but it sort of reflected Nevada. The large arched windows at the ground floor held up the bronze lions that were a symbol of

Victoria's former dominance. At the top was a flag pole that had a flag of the United States, followed by Illinois, followed by what was probably a flag of Victoria.

Unfortunately, as the town decayed, the downtown decayed faster. One by one, the businesses left as the residents packed up and moved to other suburbs. As the town reached record population lows in the 80's, whole sections of downtown closed and left empty streets for drug addicts and their dealers to roam free.

A vicious cycle emerged as the tax dollars left. The upkeep left with it and only encouraged the diaspora.

The streets were barren, the windows were smashed, and the doors were boarded up. The charm was tagged and covered up by youths disgruntled with their broken dreams. Litter collected in the corners of splintering sidewalks and busy alleyways. This section was left to rot as the inhabitants averted their attention from the anarchist free-for-all that was ironically so close to the town hall and police department.

To add to the irony, sin would be the savior of this town, for a casino with heavy tax potential was allowed into the den of wolves. Overnight, the riverboat-New Orleans themed *Titanic Thompson* made a killing, and still today gladly took the money of gambling addicts. Slowly the town had the funds to throw to hire more police, repair the streets, and entice businesses to return to the downtown. And it worked—or is working, for the cesspool dried up into a barren, but not threatening, district. Now yuppie hipsters had claimed this land with cupcake shops, live-music bars, juice bars, and bike stores. Slowly, people were walking down Victoria's streets and occasionally buying something. The area was blending the Latin and hipster cultures into a Williamsburg-Havana hybrid the town council could be proud of when they stopped resenting it.

"So how are you going to handle the lovebirds?" I asked.

"Gunshow and Laura? Well I'm going to get the larger room and they're going to get the rest of the apartment. Its sounds bad but I get my own bathroom and walk-in closet. A *big* walk in closet," God replied.

"Yeah, I guess you don't need a kitchen or anything. As long as you have your computer and a desk to hold up your diet sodas you're good."

"Hey, whatever. I'm healthy. I ate a banana this morning."

"Oh really? What did you eat yesterday?"

"Like anyone remembers what they ate yesterday."

"Well people may not remember what they ate yesterday, but at least they remembered they *did*. That's your difference."

"Jeez, Ammo you sound like my mother. Next you're going to tell me to put on makeup or get off the computer."

We were finally within sight of the apartment. It was a tall boring cement building in a complex that was probably constructed when the suburban homes were going up. After the war, families were swarming Victoria for the slice of suburbia, so entrepreneurs quickly built apartments for them to wait while their dream home was going up. They were intended to be temporary, for they were big, ugly, and made with cheap materials. They were uninteresting and uninspiring, and any description would quickly be forgotten. They looked like the backdrop for buildings in movies that refused to identify the city they were staged in.

The complex's ugliness was only emphasized by the splendid downtown just a few streets away. They were only a few stories but the skyline was clearly muddled by their presence.

We pulled up and I slithered out of the "window" of the Slag. God's door went "RRRRRRUUUUNNNNNNNNT, RRRRRRRRRUUUUUNNNNNNNNNNNT" as she got out. We walked to the back and she undid the bungee cords holding the trunk down. Inside were boxes of junk and feminine products. The only furniture was her disassembled desk, folding lawn chair, and expensive computer. I knew I was the one who was going to carry the recently cleaned, formally black desk pieces.

She grabbed a bag of clothes and I grabbed a box. She was buzzed in by Laura and we went in.

The inside had a cold war Wisconsin aesthetic with gangbanger charm woven in. The walls were wooden panels of various damage with names, nicknames, swearwords, and penises scratched in. The ceiling had a white stipple with bullet holes and spitballs surrounding cracks and water stains. The floor was a tan-brown shag that had trail marks from all of the dirty shoes that walked to and from the apartments. The common area was lit by broken and missing glass chandeliers in the entrances and little supper club wall sconces in the hallways.

The floors creaked and croaked as we journeyed up the stairs to God's third floor apartment. I looked at the wooden panels as we ascended and saw names like "Speedy", "Bloodbath", "Snowman", "Nine-Toes", and "Gumdrop". Once every few steps my shoe would sink in, leading me to assume that I was suspended only by the ruined McCarthy era carpet.

"This place is a damn mess," I finally said.

"Well we couldn't find anything in Aberdeen with Gunshow unemployed and this place actually has nice layouts so shut up. Besides it's under new management and they're going to renovate the place. I was told the new company is from LA."

"I bet a Los Angeles slum lord knows how to clean up gang violence." I said sarcastically.

"Besides, Victoria has calmed down so no new problems are going to spring up. Add that to the emerging culture here and this is going to be a good home for us. I'm actually walking distance from a venue. I get to see Little Yellow Dog on Friday and I can just walk home straight to bed."

"Lying in bed after a concert is the best feeling in the world."

"Even better than the concert itself?"

"Sometimes."

We got to her apartment, 3b (almost a never-ending pun). After some jiggling of the lock with God's key, Laura opened the door for us instead. She seemed different, less energetic with a seriousness in her eyes—like something had actually happened to her in the last five years. Looking at her burned me, so I looked at her pants, which were actually a few inches longer now.

The apartment had been updated with faux granite countertops and cheap hardwood. The walls and appliances were white with very little patina, and the widows were clean.

It was empty however, except for a bunch of dishes on the counter and a TV sitting on the floor.

"I was putting away the dishes," said Laura quietly.

"I see. Where's Gunshow?" asked God, oblivious to her emotion.

"He was hungry and went to get a few pizzas."

"I hope he shares," I said.

"Well let me show you around, Ammo," said God enthusiastically.

"Okay."

We walked past Laura in the living room and down the hallway.

"So here's the kitchen. It has a nice simple layout with rows of countertop for all your cooking needs. It has a dishwasher and fridge. Down here is their room. It's about the size of Gunshow's old room, a little smaller than mine, but of course they get priority over the living room. Here's their bathroom, easy linoleum that's already dirty from Gunshow's muddy boots. And here's my room, the walk in closet is over there with the on suite after it."

"Nice. Where do want me to put this?" I asked, indicating the box I was carrying.

"In the corner over there. I want to put some of this away. So will you go get the other things and bring them to me."

"Yes, my Goddess."

I walked out of her room and saw Laura standing and looking out the window. She had her arms folded and head tilted forward. Her hair hung down past her eyes. Her face held a thought she half understood and half didn't, but was

158

unquestionably difficult. Aside from her outfit she reminded me of her sister.

A part of me wanted to race down the stairs and happily carry up God's dirty belongings but the other half wanted to speak to the closest thing to Megan. Fortunately or unfortunately, she spoke first.

"It feels like yesterday that I would watch her out of my window, having adventures by herself in the backyard. When I was grounded in my room her little stories were the only thing that entertained me. My favorite was when she and Sunday would play detective and try to solve mysteries she came up with. She was so creative."

I rubbed my sandal on the wood floor. "Yeah."

"She had a mermaid game and would sing songs in the pool by herself. I don't get it; a pool is so boring alone." She said calmly.

I matched her calmness. "She was used to being alone. She felt safe when alone."

She had to think about that for a moment. "That's true. I couldn't stand it. I guess I only feel safe with other people."

"Yeah."

We looked at the ground together. I could feel my two halves reemerging and I was about to leave for the door when she spoke up again.

"I-I think I will visit my mother in France. Not now— not for a while—but in the future. I may not need her anymore but I owe it to my younger self to see her."

I looked out the window. "Everyone needs closure."

She looked out the window as well. "Yeah, closure."

The door busted open and Gunshow casually walked in with six pizza boxes in his hands.

"Pizza delivery for I. C. Wiener? Ha! Just fuckin' around but if you don't have any money, there's always a different way...oh hey, Ammo."

"H-hey?"

He set down the boxes and grabbed half a dozen slices. After a few chomps he spoke to me. "So come with me and we'll get the couch."

"You're not still mad at me?" I asked.

"Just come with," he replied.

He raced down the stairs and I tried to keep up. Every thunderous stomp made me a little more afraid of a stair collapse, but the wonky steps held up. As I quickly stepped behind him, I was sure the depressions in the carpet were deeper.

When I caught up to him outside, it began to rain pretty hard. I saw Gunshow already on the back of his pickup truck pushing the couch out. Each drop that crashed upon the saggy lime green upholstery increased its weight ever so slightly. And with the thousands of drops per second, carrying it up the stairs would become a difficult matter.

Gunshow decided that his rock solid muscles were enough to lift the beast. He threw down the pillows to me and preceded to lift the couch vertically into the air. Although it was impressive, he soon realized that unless he was going to drag the couch up the stairs and ruin the bottom, he was going to need my help. Temporally satisfied with himself, he set the couch down for a mortal like me to assist.

I threw the pillows back onto the couch and lifted one side. It was a heavy couch, and although I struggled, Gunshow was stone faced, pretending that my weakness wasn't satisfying him.

"So I've been doing some thinking lately, and I'm sorry I was so jealous of you," Said Gunshow. "Just because I'm a piece of shit doesn't mean you should have to be."

"You were jealous of me?" I asked.

"Yeah, well, sort of. More so I was pissed the fuck off that this awesome group of friends I had was drifting away from me. I did nothing, but everything I enjoyed about my life was falling apart around me. I realized that life is like a muscle; lifting the same weight every time is slowly going to stop muscle growth and become less and less useful. I have to keep challenging myself just to keep what I already have. So even if you go to fucking Singapore I'll take a fucking trip and hang out with you. I just want to say that I'm sorry for not pulling my weight and expecting you to do everything for me."

"Thanks, man. And I'm always going to let you crash on whatever couch I have, wherever I have it."

"Fuck yeah. And I'm not going to bitch about my problems anymore. I'm going to get a job and go to college. I just wish I thought of this shit years ago."

"I guess so, but put it this way: some people realize they're wasting their lives when they're fifty, so you didn't lose out on much."

Gunshow lifted the couch with ease while avoiding the corners of the stairs. He didn't say much for a while so I felt compelled to speak again.

"Hey, so, I'm sorry about working so much. I don't think accepting the promotion was the right answer. Whenever I wasn't with you guys or with, uh, Megan I was fucking working. It sucked as much as you thought it would."

Gunshow kept quiet for a moment, this was a good moment for an apology. "Yeah, I never fucking heard you talk about it so I just assumed you were thinking about it constantly. But yeah, I'm the idiot not you."

"We're all idiots. But I have a few days off between my last shift and my trip back to school. So, do you want to hang out, all day, like we used to?"

"Fuck yeah."

Homecoming, August 29th

I laid in my bed, waiting for the summer to end. I looked again at the posters on my wall, and they showed the hobbies and interests of some other person. A person I knew once, but now only in passing, like an old friend.

The old me was dead. I didn't die suddenly or violently, even though Megan's and Phishy's demise did change me. No, I died slowly like the Roman Empire. And like the Roman Empire, a few depreciating thoughts and feelings of my younger self still influence the biological institution that I am today.

As I gazed upon the posters, I could see the old me enjoying functions that today I wouldn't have been able to operate. I spent so much time in these video game universes that I couldn't seem to understand my own divorce from them. My friends and I played so often that our childhoods appeared to be stagnant wastes of time. But then again, a change in perception could lead anything to appear to be a waste of time.

Then why did my friends of today feel so imprisoned by their current lifestyles? They were some of the few people I knew that did whatever the hell they wanted. They lived as if they never graduated high school. Which, according to hundreds of anecdotes and countless media, was the true apple to everyone's eye.

Perhaps they could see the winding race of maturity being neck and neck throughout their lives. And now as they rest, the others in the universe are speeding past them, leaving them alone in the back.

They could have run faster—people like me were not actually that far ahead—but it's so easy to get discouraged from pulling ahead when it's the greatest time of your life. Media, friends, and especially drugs provided such a convenient way to relax.

It was in these last few weeks however, that they progressed so much further. Why now? Was it the deaths of

Megan and Phishy? Did they see that their lives were not permanent, and some sort of legacy to be remembered is important? Is it a legacy that they could never establish because they only smoked pot and hung out?

I turned in my bed. It didn't feel right for all of my friends to suddenly want some footnotes.

They lived in this perfect setting, and like all objects, they remained at rest until a force acted upon them. Only trial or trauma could sow the seeds of volition. And I had enough traumas to achieve anything.

I gazed out of my window and looked back on my childhood. I remembered Pete and I riding across the Aberdeen bike bridge with ice cream in our hands. As we stopped to carry our bikes down the steps, a bird flew by and dumped on my shoulder. We didn't think any got on my ice cream but my cookies and cream shifted from desirable to revolting. Pete laughed his ass off. Then he laughed for days, then weeks. Then in science class he would continually bring it up.

I still didn't know why he left. He didn't say or do anything; he just stopped showing up. I called and asked but he either said he was too busy or simply didn't reply. Then the slow drift apart most 19-year-olds feel left a wedge of awkwardness that only grew wider with every passing day.

He would know what to say. All I would need to say is one sentence about my situation and he would unroll a whole essay on why it happened and how to deal with it. If he was here right now, we would talk it out and nothing would be strange about it.

Well, he's only across town—a ten minute bike ride at the least. I could go outside and get on my bike and just ride over and knock on the door. And I did that—well, I did the first part.

I went to my back yard and found my bike resting against the house. It was in the same place I left it around three or four years ago. It was filthy from the dozen or so seasons it's weathered, but overall it was in good shape. Even the tires still had plenty of air. When I lifted it off the wall, I noticed the rust must have splashed onto the siding of the house after all of the rainstorms, for there was a rusty bike-shaped imprint against the house.

I was off. The wind danced around me as I pedaled faster and faster up and down the valley hills. My wheels went click-click-click every few seconds for each little crack in the old sidewalk. As I relearned my old groove, my body preemptively braced for each major fissure on the pathway. As I took each turn down the streets, my brain let go of control as the old muscle memories took over. While this journey progressed, I felt more and more comfortable doing something I should have done years ago.

I could hear the old oaks cheering me on as I passed them. The shifting winds carefully divided the overcast sky, revealing a sun I had not seen in weeks. The sun's rays casted themselves upon my body, warming it to match my mood.

I crossed over the river on Pete's bird shit bridge, bouncing dangerously down the steps as I ignored the danger they could have caused me. Geese honked loudly as I blew past them on the river walk pathway. One by one I passed the presidential streets: Tyler, Harrison, Van Buren, and Jackson. I didn't even check to see if I actually turned on JQA Ave. Like a professional athlete, I was deep in the zone.

I ran up the porch steps of 18 JQA, skipping every even numbered step as I had done since I was eight-years-old. I got to the top, opened the creaky porch door and walked into the sunroom. I took one look at the front door and stopped hard, like a car realizing the intersection was photo enforced.

I didn't know how long I stood there. Maybe a few years. The sun didn't move much though, so I would have never been able to prove it. Nothing was wrong; the door was fine. The house was fine. The only thing that wasn't fine were my thoughts. As least I assumed so, but I couldn't recall having any.

I swayed back and forth like I was waiting for a job interview, and I had the sweats to match. I was paralyzed by fear but I wasn't afraid. I was immobilized by embarrassment but I wasn't embarrassed. I was petrified by guilt but I wasn't guilty.

I had to push my arm hard against the imaginary membrane with my muscles pleading every second. I was lifting an ironclad with the finger that was only to be responsible for the doorbell, and it trembled beneath the weight. A mass of imaginary gravity distorted the universe behind me. As I reached closer and closer, the psychological vortex sucked harder and harder. Inches from the objective, the metaphysical maw absorbed everything human kind has ever understood. When the scale of distance shifted from inches to millimeters, I witnessed my parallax of existence turn reality into an incomprehensible madness of broken scientific laws. By the time I reached the crusty plastic of the doorbell, my body was metaphorically spaghettified for light years around the dark void.

I pushed. And with that action, all of my mental fabrications crashed around me in an apocalyptic firestorm of an incredible magnitude. With each ding something exploded between my neurons. When the annoying jingle was over, I muttered, "Deep in the heart of Tex-uuusss," under my breath for the 60,000th time.

See You Later, August 26th

"Hey, Brian. The party's already started," said Laura.

"Great. I bought a case of beer," I replied.

"Oh I'll take that, come on in and grab a drink."

I walked into God's apartment. Which I should consider God's, Gunshow's, and Laura's, but it wasn't like I didn't know who was in charge of the place.

The living room to my left had two old, unmatching couches along the wall of the exit door. One was the lime green situation I helped bring up and the other was a conjoined tan suede recliner with receding hairline levels of suede. On the intersecting wall was the window with various candles, vases, and pictures of Gunshow and Laura on the windowsill. Next to that was a dumbbell set that started at 50 lbs. and went to 200 lbs. It looked old and a few of the bells were missing. Intersecting that wall was a half-assed computer desk enveloped in an aggressive ball of wires. A computer and monitor were there too but they looked like they couldn't be reached through the tangles. Next to that was an old 55" flat screen TV sitting on the floor. I knew from personal experience that it had been missing a remote for at least ten years and stickers of various games from various ages still covered the sides. Above the TV hung a banner that said "Farewell Brian and William!" with an "& Jerry" sticky note beneath it.

Hanging out in the living room was Jerry, Gunshow, and Nik. I decided to jump into their conversation first.

"So what's going to be your first stop again?" asked Nik.

Jerry tilted his head back and folded his arms. I seemed he liked answering questions he'd already answered. "Well now I'm thinking of Des Moines instead of Madison. I don't know what's out there but I'm going to start small before I hit up Denver and Vegas and Los Angeles,"

"Shit, bro. Aren't you afraid of getting robbed or some shit?" asked Gunshow.

Jerry laughed. "Robbed of what? Old clothes? Old van? The nicest thing I got is a knock-off brand mp3 player from high school. I guess they could snatch the sticky quarters from my change cup."

Gunshow looked over at Laura, who was putting a cake in the oven. "Yeah, well I couldn't enjoy traveling alone,"

Jerry shook his head in disbelief. "Ya'know, everybody tells me that."

"You're so lucky. I have no money to do that," said Nik as he spit on the floor and rubbed it out with his shoe.

Jerry brushed his hair back very slowly. "It's actually pretty cheap. I only saved up 5 grand and that should last me more than a year. If you got a place to sleep like I do then all you really need to pay for is booze, food, and fun."

"Cool. I'm going to get a van and me and my boys are gunna hit the road," said Nik.

I scoffed at his statement. "Well first you need money, and that requires a job,"

"Shut up, Ammo. I'm getting a job. I'm going to work at Clatcher." He stepped back but leaned forward like he was ready to fight.

"Doing what?" I asked. "Putting the caps on shoelaces? Adding glue to envelope flaps? Sticking the cap on ball point pens?"

He made the same pouty face I've seen since I met him. "Why do you have to be so mean to me? It's a shitty job but it'll pay me for what I want to do. Besides, you work at a grocery store. Do you want paper or plastic?"

"For your information, I was a manager so people would come to me *demanding* paper or plastic. Thank God my last day was yesterday. But knowing Raj he'll ask me to come in while I'm at school."

"Fucking old hags. They always wanted plastic because that's what Hitler gave them when he was a bag boy for them in Camelot," said Gunshow angrily.

"Camelot's in England," said Jerry.

167

Gunshow took a gulp of his drink. "So? It's a fucking joke. Fine, when Hitler was a bag boy in Australia."

"Man, Gunshow, you're so dumb," Laughed Nik.

He took a few more gulps. "At least I graduated High school. And had a job. And a girlfriend. And can buy my own fucking weed."

"You're an asshole," he replied.

Knowing that this conversation was about to get cyclical, I decided to move on to the next group.

I causally walked past the kitchen when I noticed Theodora talking to Laura. I scurried ahead to avoid the aggressive jailbait; the last thing I wanted now was a leech draining me of all of my social interaction. Luckily, her back was to me so I could easily slip past.

I entered God's room. There was a messy bed in the corner with pulled off sheets and ruffled pillows. It was facing an old dresser with an older bulky television resting on top of it. Next to the TV was a wide assortment of beauty products ranging from half used perfumes to half used lotion to half used makeup. Emanating from her closet was clothing dumped across the floor in such a way that some sort of fabric grenade must have gone off.

Sitting on the floor in a circle was Dan, Will, God, and Alex. I decided to try my luck and sit on the bed.

"So you mentioned you wanted to leave, but what made you decide to leave *now*?" asked God half buzzed.

"Well, I always had it on the back of my mind. I really like the culture of Japan and I want to be an avant-garde architect, and what better place to be then Japan," replied William-san informatively.

"What do you mean by avant-garde? They have crazy buildings in Japan?" she asked slowly and curiously.

Like a robot he replied. "Of course. Since everything was destroyed in the Second World War, buildings needed to be made fast to give everyone a place to live. This meant that the quality was terrible. People knew this because the buildings were only meant to stick around until the better buildings with more time and care could be built. However, the public perception shifted and new equaled better. Add in the fact that everything new in Japan is generally praised and that creates a culture of constantly rebuilding homes. Knowing that each house is only going to stand for about a decade, people are more interested in living in unique homes."

"I always thought you'd be more into a craft like animation than architecture," I said.

"Well, I was always mesmerized by the skyscrapers in Chicago. That led my interest in architecture."

"But weren't you really into anime and manga?" I asked.

He laughed "Yes, I'm a huge fan and I'd probably end up in Japan teaching English or something without my degree."

"So what are you more interested in about moving to Japan? Anime or architecture?" asked God with a little more buzz.

Finally some enthusiasm entered his speech. "Both. I loved them separately and when I discovered that I could bring them together I lost my mind. I knew I had to go."

"But, so why now?" She asked.

"Oh yeah, I guess I didn't answer the question. I don't know really. The timing just felt right."

"I was in Japan," said Dan like a personified puppy.

"Really? I didn't know this. Was it for the air force?" God asked with faked interest.

Dan grew a huge smile. "Yeah, it was a lot of fun."

We waited for him to say more but he seemed to drift off into old memories. His eyes glazed over with feelings of importance and meaning. He saw parties and adventure with the comradery of the military. He saw cute Japanese girls flirting with him and asking about the marvelous wonders of America. He looked back to a place that had him set in the right groove and offered him the structure that was desired of a man that was seldom motivated to do anything.

God could barely hold her unenthusiasm. "What did you do there, Dan?"

Dan was so excited with the fact that he was mildly interesting. "Everything. I used to fly planes over China, but I'm not supposed to tell anyone that."

"That's fine. no one would believe you anyway. Like how you wrote poems," I said a little bit too snarky.

Dan's good mood flat lined. "Wh-what? Y-you know about my p-poems?"

"Dan, don't be embarrassed. They're so thoughtful. I think we all might have respected you more after we read them," said God incredibly mother like.

Dan began to hyperventilate. "*We*? Does everyone know?"

"Yes, but don't feel bad; they're great."

He guzzled down his beer and got up to get a few dozen more. It looks like he might do his thriller dance tonight.

"I feel bad for him, but he should be proud of his work," declared God.

"Did he tell you he's getting his license?" asked Will calmly.

"No, he rarely tells anyone anything," I said.

"Yeah, he told me in the car when I picked him up. He wanted me to teach him but I'm leaving, so he's looking for a mentor. Gunshow might teach him but I don't think it's a good idea for him to learn how to drive like a car bomber," said Will.

"I could teach him. We're practically neighbors now that I live in Victoria. Wow, that's so weird to say. I'm a Victorian, not a girl living in her parent's house. V-i-c-t-o-r-i-a-n," said God in glorious amazement.

Alex said something at this point but it probably didn't matter.

"Yeah, it's been a few days. So how's independent life?" I asked.

Still on her independence kick, she said: "Awesome. I can do whatever I want whenever I want."

"You did that before though. I don't even think you had a curfew," I said.

"I know, but now I don't have a mother constantly yelling at me. And with siblings bothering me at every step. I'm free."

Alex said another pointless thing.

"What about the apartment itself?" asked Will.

"Well, I'm against my roommates' décor," she replied, "but that's part of the agreement. Otherwise this place is a great home in a great location. The only strange thing is that my balcony access is through my closet."

"I didn't know you had a balcony. Can I see it?" I asked inquisitively.

"Yeah, go right ahead. There's nothing out there though." She said somewhat confused.

"That's fine. I just want to get a look at the moonlight."

"Okay, but don't stay out too long. Laura dirtied every pot, utensil, and counter making you guys a going away cake."

"That sounds good. What flavor is it?"

God laughed a little. "Let's just say your mileage may vary depending on what slice you get."

"What?" asked a confused Will.

God laughed a little harder. "She couldn't decide on a flavor so she mixed several boxes together. I refused to sample it."

It *was* a weird set up. Inside the jungle of the God's clothing was a door that looked a little too small. The floor didn't change and there was no paneling so there was no indication that the balcony door should exist.

Outside the air was cool, but not too cool to need a jacket. It was dark, since there was no porch light so the only illumination came from the full moon that gave shape to the world below. Without any details, all I could see were little lights around the complex that twinkled like little stars. I could see bodies pass between and beneath them, but nothing I could identify. In the dark areas of the lawn, I could see a mist slowly encroaching upon the area.

I looked at the downtown from the corner of the balcony and saw drunkards dancing with delight, singing a tune I was too far away to hear. There were people walking and

171

couples watching the river from the guardrail of the river walk. A few cars passed by and went down the lightly illuminated suburban streets.

On the other side was the remarkably dark Drag Woods. Beyond that were the little twinkles of light from the old smokestacks in Aberdeen. On the hill beyond those was an exceptionally dark void that must have been Graham Manor.

It was quiet; just what I wanted. I could hear cars in the distance, but their gentle passing created a calming melody that I'm sure was preferable to complete silence. As I focused on the sounds, I heard the animals of the river: frogs croaked, bugs chirped, and an owl hoooo in the distance. United, this symphony of the Aberdeen Valley nightlife calmed me and allowed me to patch a few of the holes left in my mind from the recently departed in my life.

"Hello, Brian."

Dammit. That innocently high pitched voice could only come from one person.

"What is it, Theodora?"

I turned and saw the littlest Pelio kid with a smile so wide it showed all of her braces. She must have felt that her sister was mature or something because she was wearing a band shirt with God's staple tight black jeans.

"I heard you were here and I wanted to see you because I'm so sorry your friends Phishy and Megan died I want you to know that I'm here for you and I want you to be okay because you don't deserve to be so sad because you're such a nice person." She needed to breathe heavily after that.

"Okay, thank you…"

"When my Grandpa died I was so sad and I'm sorry." Her nerves fluttered around the balcony and choked out whatever calmness was giving me peace.

Her feelings must have been too new to properly speak to me, so I had to steer the conversation away from whatever the sluttiest of her friends told her about.

"You in school?" Which was the most obvious answer anyone could ask a 14-year-old.

172

"Yeah, I go to Aberdeen-Victoria High in two weeks. I'm going to be a freshman."

It worked out. She went from that weird empty gaze to a calmer yet still interested one. It was the first crack in an undesired cult of personality. Hopefully this year she would discover a new boy to fixate on and I could be free.

After some long gazing, her eyes turned towards the ground, as she realized I too must be leaving.

She leaned next to me, along the railing I too was leaning on. "So you are going back to school too?" she asked.

"Yeah, I leave on Thursday. Back to the corn fields, and away from this universe."

"That must be nice for you. I bet you want to leave this place behind." She said apologetically.

"Well I do now, but only to clear my head. When I came back this summer I was convinced that I was going to leave this pond of stagnant relationships into a world that could make my dreams come true. Now I see that I unfairly blamed this valley for my fears. I realize now that I don't have to forsake my past for my future. I can hold onto the people I care about here."

"Wow, was all that from Phishy's and Megan's death?"

"No, but they helped me see what was right in front of me. I will carry them with me though, as people who existed in a past life, and who I owe a meaning to their demise. I don't know if there was a purpose to their death, but I will find purpose to their memories."

"Oh, Brian. You're so deep and thoughtful."

"Everyone is full of thoughts, but seldom few share the ones they're not sure others will understand."

She was silent, trying to see if her Shakespeare was implying something about her. It didn't matter though because Laura distracted her by opening the balcony door.

"What are you doing out here? Come on in and get some cake!" she said half buzzed.

We returned to the living room with Gunshow holding the cake and God standing on the lime green couch shushing everyone. Eventually everyone listened and quieted down.

"Now along with a house warming party, this is also a going away party. And I want the people disembarking from us soon to have a piece to say to us before we end the night. I want the three gentlemen up here with me," declared God.

Jerry, Will, and I stood up on the couch in that order and gazed at everyone like pageant contestants.

God motioned Jerry to speak as she stepped off her pulpit. He cleared his throat and adjusted his invisible tie before he spoke. "I want everyone to know that you're all the best. You guys started out as my clients but quickly became my friends. And thanks to all your drug money, I'm going to travel North America until I get sick of it—or more likely when the party van breaks down. If you see the van with the three wolves howling at the moon on the side, you come down and light up with me for free. And if you happen to see a gutter punk chick around my arm, don't mention her smell and just go with it."

With that, he hopped down as the audience—and especially Nik—cheered for him. It took a moment before they were ready for Will.

"I started out as a spotter for Gunshow in excel gym, and ended up standing on this couch telling you guys how much I'm going to miss you all. I don't know if any of you will ever find yourselves in Japan, but know if you do then there's always an ice cold plate of sushi waiting for ya. When I have my own architect firm, give me a call and I'll design a home for you guys at a tremendously low discount. And if you happen to meet my future lady and she asks about your blood type, just go with it. It's a Japanese thing."

Will jumped down and was handed a slice of cake by Laura. I then noticed Jerry got one too. Dan patted him on the back a little too hard, but Will either didn't notice or was simply being polite to a man who couldn't possibly control his jealousy.

Then they all looked at me. I was mentally preparing my speech, and I decided to sort of follow the trend.

"So I've been with all of you since the beginning. Pete and I formed this group back in grade school, and one by one you all joined in because we were so cool, but mostly for geographic reasons. And I see you guys, and I know this is sincerely the greatest group of people I will ever meet. So I want everyone to raise their glasses and plastics and propose a toast to whatever the fuck we did, whatever the fuck we're doing, and wherever the fuck we're going. You guys. You guys gave me so many fantastic life experiences I will cherish to the grave. And even though a few are no longer with us, I want them to live on in the stories we tell our children and grandchildren. I want them to make us smile and laugh for the next thousand years. I want them to be alive in our hearts, because I know that's what they would want from us.

But this party's about the living, and I want each and every one of you to live it up tonight, because it will be the last time for a while.

Oh yeah, and if you meet my girlfriend, mind your manners I guess? Really I mean this for Gunshow."

"Fucking never!" he replied.

I hopped down and shook some hands like a politician. Laura meandered through the crowd and handed me my cake. Mintostrawcletmallow, my favorite.

The group began to talk loudly as Laura passed out her Franken-food. A few enjoyed it.

God snuck around the crowd and grabbed me by the shoulders. She leaned in and whispered in my ear, "I think it's time for a 'thrilling' presentation, if you know what I mean."

"Sure thing, but I left my skull at home. I could ask Gunshow to make one for us."

"No, dummy. A 'Dantastic' moment."

I laughed a little. "Oh, do you think he is at a perfect alcoholic saturation?"

"I think so. He had four beers—just enough but not too far."

"Well then *OOOW*!"

She knew what that meant, and she returned into the midst of the crowd.

Gunshow walked up to me with his usual drunken stomp. Pedro Cali swished out of its bottle, which was quite impressive considering that it was almost empty. "Bro, fucking awesome speech. You need to speak at my wedding, but you're going to half to make sure you zneak in a few roars," he carefully mushed out.

"Why roars?"

"Becauze I'm going to bang a lion and I don't want her to feel left out."

"Why a lion? What about Laura?"

"Becauze I need a kid who is betterer than me, and zince I'm the strongest man alive its only logic-ca-cle that I bang a lion. For the extra livez—he'll at least get like, 5. And I have to marry her becauze I don't want a bastard becauze then he couldn't have the landz I, uh, conquered."

"What about Laura?"

"Well, she can hang out and be my mizztreztzezz, a dezzpot always needz a zide biznich. Like that roman guy wid da zalad. He had bizniches"

Suddenly, God snuck over to the stereo and changed the music from electronica to a song with a creepy door opening and a wolf howling in the background. One by one, we quieted down until only Dan was left talking about a new tangerine anime to Will. It wasn't until an 80's synthesizer blared a very fake trumpet sound that Dan knew his fate.

All through the breakdown he refused, politely, and then a little more assertively (as assertive Dan could be). He kept saying no until Michael Jackson sang, *"It's close to midnight,"* and then POW! Dan jumped to the middle of the floor, body ready. He moved so fast, so automatically that I knew a different being was in control of this man's body. A being that Dan kept deep down inside; a man that passionately loved to express, a man that could only escape after five shots of Pedro Cali, a man who couldn't stop the *Thriller*.

He did not move. He glided across the floor in perfectly choreographed spins, leans, and lurches. The music sunk him into a synchronized machine that captivated any viewer with a human obsession of melodic complexity. As the song beat along, he timed sips of his alcohol, yet his execution appeared to be unfazed by the inebriation.

It wasn't until the chorus that we all joined in. Not to dance with Dan, but to simply shake along and sing. We reserved our movements to compliment the gentle giant kicking it on center stage. God sang the rest of the lines, for the rest of us only knew this tune in a drunken passing. However, the veterans of this spectacle knew the words that the backup dancers sang along to, and we preceded to do our part in the performance. Dan preferred the King of Pop's voice and respectfully lip-synced each word as if they were his own. He didn't need to speak; his passion and energy were expressed perfectly on his face.

After a few minutes in, Dan was too hot for his shirt and exposed his rather unpleasant pale beer gut, his doughy flesh jiggling with every sway. The shockwaves eventually resembled a consistent rumble between each major flap of the belly.

Laura placed one of her trilby hats on Dan's head, but he grabbed it flawlessly in motion and threw it on the ground.

"THAT'S FUCKING SMOOTH CRIMINAL!" he yelled with passion, not rage.

However, not even Gunshow could withstand the .5 alcohol level coursing through Dan's veins. Dan began to fumble and lose time when the old man spoke his poppy chant. But we were determined for this to be a Thriller performance he would finish, and we all began to chant *Dan! Dan! Dan!*

That helped him maintain composure. However, as the song escalated at the end, Dan fumbled harder and harder, so we cheered him on as he struggled to stay afloat.

As his balance failed we didn't believe he could make it, but then the song cut right at the end. He made it! He did a full Thriller play through, but he was on the ground before the laughter ended.

Me and Gunshow helped him up, and we all cheered him like he came home from the war. The smiles on our faces were wide, but the smile on his face was wider.

Deep in the Heart, August 29th

When I opened my eyes, I saw Pete's mother staring at me through the doorway. "Wow, Brian. It's been a long time since I've seen you," she said.

"Hello, Mrs. Gomez. Is Pete here?" I asked like the ten-year-old I was channeling.

She laughed a bit. "Shoot, Brian. You're old enough to drink. Call me Heather."

"Okay," I said as I rubbed my shoe on the stoop.

"But yeah, Pete is in his room. I think he's playing a game or something."

Heather returned to the backyard and left me alone. She was splitting logs for the big fire pit. I watched her for a while because my mind was too nervous to do anything else. After some time, it became too strange to just stare, so I looked around the house to build confidence.

The place hadn't changed in fourteen years (except for the TV). The walls were a light stained wood with smokehouse levels of Texan memorabilia on the walls. Three Lone Star flags in the state shape, an actual Lone Star flag behind the TV, nine old beer logos, a cow skull, six posters of western movies, a Texas license plate, two Cowboys jerseys, several snake skins, two buck heads, and finally, an A&M flag.

The furniture was made of logs—not wood, but logs. The bark was covered in some laminating chemicals but years of things bumping into it (myself included) had worn the veneer away. The coffee tables, the end tables, the lamps, the TV stand, and even the sides of the couches were made from this sort of petrified wood. The couch cushions themselves had an elaborate Pueblo-like design commonly found on salsa bottles. In the center of it all was the chandelier of deer antlers. The lights were large Christmas lights so most of the lighting was dependent upon the steer horn lights with cowhide shades on either side of the couches. I headed down the hallway to get closer to Pete's room.

The hallway had several dozen gun racks with various rifles hanging upon them. They varied in age from 1888 to 2009 and one was allegedly from the revolutionary war, which I doubted. I spent a lot of time looking at these guns while I waited for Pete to get ready for our hangouts. I walked past the nautical themed bathroom that faced a "Don't Mess With Texas" poster. I checked and the poster still had the gum Phishy left behind it back in middle school.

Pete's bedroom door still had the "little rangers" photo. It was a photograph of 12-year-old Gunshow, me, Pete, Phishy, and God. We were celebrating Pete's birthday and of course his mother was making him wear a little A&M jersey. We were all smiling so hard and having a wonderful time. This poster was at eye level, so he must have seen this thing every day.

I was so nervous before, but now that I was amongst the pieces of my past, it made me feel a little safer. I wouldn't go as far as to say that I was confident, but this immersion allowed me to unconsciously move to my old best friend's room. Even without speaking to him, I already felt more at ease. I felt like I stepped off a boat from a long voyage, and my salt wife was running to embrace me in her arms.

I knew I was trembling, but it wasn't apparent until I grabbed the doorknob. It was loose from when we tried to pull God's tooth out sitcom style. Needless to say, God's fangs were stronger than Taiwanese engineering and ten year olds shouldn't fix machines. The wobbling eased with my memories, so I reflected on all the times Gunshow hung his leather jacket on the knob only to have it fall under the weight.

It was a success. Before I even realized it I opened the door to Pete lying on his bunk bed playing a video game. He quickly glanced at me before he went back to the mission.

"Hey, Ammo," he said.

"Hey," I mumbled.

"What's up?" he said with clearly more interest in his game

"Phishy died."

179

"I know, I was at his funeral."

"Really? So were we. How come we didn't see you?"

"I was going to talk to you guys but ya'll were already pounding the sauce. I thought that was kind of rude so I left."

His game finished and he tossed the controller on the bed. He took off his headset and scratched his long sleek black hair before he looked at me.

"I can't believe he's gone," I said.

"I know. I'm going to miss that sneaky bastard."

"Did you know who killed him?"

His head turned and his eyes half squinted. He didn't know what I was going to say but he knew it was important. He began to stroke his wiry goatee, just like he always did to prepare for my chains of bizarre information.

"I heard it was a cop. Drove up and shot him, I think. Why do you ask that Ammo?" His voice got low, the kind of low that made it socially acceptable to talk about serious and/or dark topics.

"That's true. His name was Adam Foster. I dated his daughter, Megan Foster."

"Megan… Megan. Did we go to high school with her?"

"Yeah, she was white with long brown hair. She always wore white sweaters with an oversized backpack."

"Oh yeah, she was my science partner freshman year. I called her Ghost because she never said a word, and when she did it was always so strange. She got mad when I told her to relax all the time. So why is she more than an ex?" He ended on a suspicious note.

"She uh, passed away. Killed herself. I think Adam blamed Phishy for her death."

He leaned back in his bunk bed. The shadow from the top bunk concealed his body so all I could see were his hairy gangly legs sticking out of his Aberdeen-Victoria High gym shorts.

"Wow, I mean, I didn't know her too well but hell. What did Phishy do?"

"Nothing, he was just an ass at her wake. I think Mr. Foster just wanted a suspect."

He leaned back into the light and exposed his long face and skinny, hairy, tan body.

"Damn," he whispered.

"Yeah," I replied.

"I'm sorry for your losses. Is this why you came by? Do you want to go get something to eat or something?"

"No. I'm good."

"Uh, okay then. Do you want to play video games?"

"Why did you leave?" I snapped.

"What do you mean? Where did I go?" he asked defensively.

He should be on the defensive, because the confusion and frustration from my best friend avoiding me for three years flipped from anxiety to anger. I clenched my fists and stepped over to him.

"You know what I mean! I haven't seen you since the graduation party! We called you for months and you blew us off every time. You dropped off the face of the Earth and I want to know why!"

He stood up to meet me at eye level. "I left because you guys were becoming drug addict losers and I wanted no part of your bullshit. Throughout senior year you guys experimented with harder and harder junk and wanted to do less and less because of it. Do you even remember that party? You guys were in the basement smoking weed and watching rerun cartoons while 50 people were in the backyard having a good time! You want to know why that was the last time you guys saw me? Because I made a promise to myself that if ya'll were not going to take any initiative with anything then I wasn't going to force anything with you guys. I wasn't going to hang out with you guys until at least one of you came by and asked what the hell was up with me. It may have taken three years but now one of you finally did it."

I shook my head in disbelief. "That's so petty. We even called and texted you for months!"

"That sort of contact is cheap—so cheap that I still consider it ignoring the situation. I needed more proof that you guys were still motivated to do anything."

I shrugged my shoulders. "Well, I'm here now."

"Yeah, and now we can resume our friendship. It's not like I wanted to stop being friends with you guys. I just was waiting out your pathetic drug experimentation phase."

"After years of pointlessness," I said in a way so passive aggressively that Megan's corpse turned with jealousy.

"I agree," he said in earnest.

I sat down on his bed, but Pete remained standing. He combed back his black greasy hair with his hand. I looked down at the floor. I could see the little holes left by Phishy when he used to poke things with his butterfly knife he got in Chicago.

"I was expecting a few months. I was expecting to sled with you guys down Blood Mountain again on my first winter break. I was excited to crash into a foot of snow after the perpetual heat from what is allegedly autumn in Texas," said Pete.

If Gunshow were in this position instead of me then at this point he would have punched Pete in the face. If it were God she would have kept yelling and throwing evidence at him until she let herself out. If it were Phishy he would have spun every conversation around to make Pete the bad guy. Instead it was me. And here I was sitting on his bed actually listening to him and choosing to not say a word.

I was the only one who could be reasoned with. It was me who could actually see his point and finally become self-aware enough to evaluate myself. I was also the only one who had any willpower left to see him, and I was pretty sure he knew that.

"Why are we like this?" I asked.

"We who? Like me and you? Our group?"

"No, humans. I can see this in all of us. I rarely see anyone actively trying to solve their problems or achieve anything. I see people like Megan and old classmates, and hell, even everyday people doing nothing even though we all can clearly see what needs to be done. I mean, it took the deaths of a girl I was close with and one of my best friends just to visit someone I didn't see as having a problem with. It seems to me that we need to suffer to truly achieve anything."

"No, inspiration and motivation come from mindsets—same as apathy and procrastination," he said. "We need to change our minds in order to change our lives. The reason you see suffering as the sole catalyst for anything is because it is so easily able to change us. The very brightness of our lives will blind the paths in front of us, but evaluating our perceptions can be an adequate lens to see where we are heading.

I didn't leave because I was giving up on you guys. Everything I said was ignored, so I thought my absence would wake you guys up. Now that you're here I see that I was correct."

I rubbed my sandal against the bed post. Just above my foot was the horrible portrait of Pete God painted when she was into art. The little wibbly-wobbly lines allowed me to reflect on what he said. At the beginning of the summer I would have heard none of his philosophy, but now I could see his point.

"The others have changed too," I said. "They're finally doing what they've been talking about since high school. You should come back with me. I can show you God's apartment."

"Well it's got to be today. Tomorrow I fly back to college."

"Perfect."

www.ingramcontent.com/pod-product-compliance
Lightning Source LLC
Chambersburg PA
CBHW031956040426
42448CB00006B/387